WORLD ENGLISH Intro

SECOND EDITION

Real People • Real Places • Real Language

Martin Milner, Author

Rob Jenkins, Series Editor

Australia • Brazil • Japan • Korea • Mexico • Singapore • Spain • United Kingdom • United States

World English Intro
Real People, Real Places, Real Language
Martin Milner, Author
Rob Jenkins, Series Editor

Publisher: Sherrise Roehr

Executive Editor: Sarah Kenney

Senior Development Editor: Margarita Matte

Development Editor: Brenden Layte

Assistant Editor: Alison Bruno

Editorial Assistant: Patricia Giunta

Media Researcher: Leila Hishmeh

Senior Technology Product Manager: Scott Rule

Director of Global Marketing: Ian Martin

Senior Product Marketing Manager:
    Caitlin Thomas

Sr. Director, ELT & World Languages:
    Michael Burggren

Production Manager: Daisy Sosa

Content Project Manager: Andrea Bobotas

Senior Print Buyer: Mary Beth Hennebury

Cover Designer: Aaron Opie

Art Director: Scott Baker

Creative Director: Chris Roy

Cover Image: Martin Roemers/Panos Pictures

Compositor: MPS Limited

Cover image

Trams, food vendors, and pedestrians in Taksim Square, Central Istanbul, Turkey

World English Intro ISBN: 978-1-285-84868-6
World English Intro + CD-ROM ISBN: 978-1-285-84834-1
World English Intro + Online Workbook ISBN: 978-1-305-08955-6

National Geographic Learning
20 Channel Center Street
Boston, MA 02210
USA

Cengage Learning is a leading provider of customized learning solutions with office locations around the globe, including Singapore, the United Kingdom, Australia, Mexico, Brazil, and Japan.

Cengage Learning products are represented in Canada by Nelson Education, Ltd.

Visit National Geographic Learning online at **ngl.cengage.com**

Visit our corporate website at **www.cengage.com**

Printed in China
5 6 7 21 20

Thank you to the educators who provided invaluable feedback during the development of the second edition of the *World English* series:

AMERICAS

Brazil

Renata Cardoso, Universidade de Brasília, Brasília
Gladys De Sousa, Universidade Federal de Minas Gerais, Belo Horizonte
Marilena Fernandes, Associação Alumni, São Paulo
Mary Ruth Popov, Ingles Express, Ltda., Belo Horizonte
Ana Rosa, Speed, Vila Velha
Danny Sheps, English4u2, Natal
Renata Zainotte, Go Up Idiomas, Rio de Janeiro

Colombia

Eida Caicedo, Universidad de San Buenaventura Cali, Cali
Andres Felipe Echeverri Patiño, Corporación Universitaria Lasallista, Envigado
Luz Libia Rey, Centro Colombo Americano, Bogota

Dominican Republic

Aida Rosales, Instituto Cultural Dominico-Americano, Santo Domingo

Ecuador

Elizabeth Ortiz, COPEI-Copol English Institute, Guayaquil

Mexico

Ramon Aguilar, LEC Languages and Education Consulting, Hermosillo
Claudia García-Moreno Ávila, Universidad Autónoma del Estado de México, Toluca
Ana María Benton, Universidad Anahuac Mexico Norte, Huixquilucan
Martha Del Angel, Tecnológico de Monterrey, Monterrey
Sachenka García B., Universidad Kino, Hermosillo
Cinthia I. Navarrete García, Universidad Autónoma del Estado de México, Toluca
Alonso Gaxiola, Universidad Autonoma de Sinaloa, Guasave
Raquel Hernandez, Tecnológico de Monterrey, Monterrey
Beatriz Cuenca Hernández, Universidad Autónoma del Estado de México, Toluca
Luz María Lara Hernández, Universidad Autónoma del Estado de México, Toluca
Esthela Ramírez Hernández, Universidad Autónoma del Estado de México, Toluca
Ma Guadalupe Peña Huerta, Universidad Autónoma del Estado de México, Toluca
Elsa Iruegas, Prepa Tec Campus Cumbres, Monterrey
María del Carmen Turral Maya, Universidad Autónoma del Estado de México, Toluca
Lima Melani Ayala Olvera, Universidad Autónoma del Estado de México, Toluca
Suraya Ordorica Reyes, Universidad Autónoma del Estado de México, Toluca
Leonor Rosales, Tecnológico de Monterrey, Monterrey
Leticia Adelina Ruiz Guerrero, ITESO, Jesuit University, Tlaquepaque

United States

Nancy Alaks, College of DuPage, Glen Ellyn, IL
Annette Barker, College of DuPage, Aurora, IL
Joyce Gatto, College of Lake County, Grayslake, IL
Donna Glade-Tau, Harper College, Palatine, IL
Mary "Katie" Hu, Lone Star College – North Harris, Houston, TX
Christy Naghitorabi, University of South Florida, St. Petersburg, FL

ASIA

Beri Ali, Cleverlearn (American Academy), Ho Chi Minh City
Ronald Anderson, Chonnam National University, Yeosu Campus, Jeollanam
Michael Brown, Canadian Secondary Wenzhou No. 22 School, Wenzhou
Leyi Cao, Macau University of Science and Technology, Macau
Maneerat Chuaychoowong, Mae Fah Luang University, Chiang Rai
Sooah Chung, Hwarang Elementary School, Seoul
Edgar Du, Vanung University, Taoyuan County
David Fairweather, Asahikawa Daigaku, Asahikawa
Andrew Garth, Chonnam National University, Yeosu Campus, Jeollanam
Brian Gaynor, Muroran Institute of Technology, Muroran-shi
Emma Gould, Chonnam National University, Yeosu Campus, Jeollanam
David Grant, Kochi National College of Technology, Nankoku
Michael Halloran, Chonnam National University, Yeosu Campus, Jeollanam
Nina Ainun Hamdan, University Malaysia, Kuala Lumpur
Richard Hatcher, Chonnam National University, Yeosu Campus, Jeollanam
Edward Tze-Lu Ho, Chihlee Institute of Technology, New Taipei City
Soontae Hong, Yonsei University, Seoul
Chaiyathip Katsura, Mae Fah Luang University, Chiang Rai
Byoung-Kyo Lee, Yonsei University, Seoul
Han Li, Aceleader International Language Center, Beijing
Michael McGuire, Kansai Gaidai University, Osaka
Yu Jin Ng, Universiti Tenaga Nasional, Kajang, Selangor
Somaly Pan, Royal University of Phnom Penh, Phnom Penh
HyunSuk Park, Halla University, Wonju
Bunroeun Pich, Build Bright University, Phnom Penh
Renee Sawazaki, Surugadai University, Annaka-shi
Adam Schofield, Cleverlearn (American Academy), Ho Chi Minh City
Pawadee Srisang, Burapha University, Chanthaburi Campus, Ta-Mai District
Douglas Sweetlove, Kinjo Gakuin University, Nagoya
Tari Lee Sykes, National Taiwan University of Science and Technology, Taipei
Monika Szirmai, Hiroshima International University, Hiroshima
Sherry Wen, Yan Ping High School, Taipei
Chris Wilson, Okinawa University, Naha City, Okinawa
Christopher Wood, Meijo University, Nagoya
Evelyn Wu, Minghsin University of Science and Technology, Xinfeng, Hsinchu County
Aroma Xiang, Macau University of Science and Technology, Macau
Zoe Xie, Macau University of Science and Technology, Macau
Juan Xu, Macau University of Science and Technology, Macau
Florence Yap, Chang Gung University, Taoyuan
Sukanda Yatprom, Mae Fah Luang University, Chiang Rai
Echo Yu, Macau University of Science and Technology, Macau

The publisher would like to extend a special thank you to Raúl Billini, English Coordinator, Mi Colegio, Dominican Republic, for his contributions to the series.

BACKGROUND – LEARNING AND INSTRUCTION

Learning has been described as acquiring knowledge. Obtaining knowledge does not guarantee understanding, however. A math student, for example, could replicate any number of algebraic formulas, but never come to an *understanding* of how they could be used or for what purpose he or she has learned them. If understanding is defined as the ability to use knowledge, then learning could be defined differently and more accurately. The ability of the student to use knowledge instead of merely receiving information therefore becomes the goal and the standard by which learning is assessed.

This revelation has led to classrooms that are no longer teacher-centric or lecture driven. Instead, students are asked to think, ponder, and make decisions based on the information received or, even more productive, students are asked to construct learning or discover information in personal pursuits, or with help from an instructor, with partners, or in groups. The practice they get from such approaches stimulates learning with a purpose. The purpose becomes a tangible goal or objective that provides opportunities for students to transfer skills and experiences to future learning.

In the context of language development, this approach becomes essential to real learning and understanding. Learning a language is a skill that is developed only after significant practice. Students can learn the mechanics of a language but when confronted with real-world situations, they are not capable of communication. Therefore, it might be better to shift the discussion from "Language Learning" to "Communication Building." Communication should not be limited to only the productive skills. Reading and listening serve important avenues for communication as well.

FOUR PRINCIPLES TO DEVELOPING LEARNING ENVIRONMENTS

Mission: The goal or mission of a language course might adequately be stated as the pursuit of providing sufficient information and practice to allow students to communicate accurately and effectively to a reasonable extent given the level, student experiences, and time on task provided. This goal can be reflected in potential student learning outcomes identified by what students will be able to do through performance indicators.

World English provides a clear chart within the table of contents to show the expected outcomes of the course. The books are designed to capture student imagination and allow students ample opportunities to communicate. A study of the table of contents identifies the process of communication building that will go on during the course.

Context: It is important to identify what vehicle will be used to provide instruction. If students are to learn through practice, language cannot be introduced as isolated verb forms, nouns, and modifiers. It must have context. To reach the learners and to provide opportunities to communicate, the context must be interesting and relevant to learners' lives and expectations. In other words, there must be a purpose and students must have a clear understanding of what that purpose is.

World English provides a meaningful context that allows students to connect with the world. Research has demonstrated pictures and illustrations are best suited for creating interest and motivation within learners. National Geographic has a long history of providing magnificent learning environments through pictures, illustrations, true accounts, and video. The pictures, stories, and video capture the learners' imagination and "hook" them to learning in such a way that students have significant reasons to communicate promoting interaction and critical thinking. The context will also present students with a desire to know more, leading to life-long learning.

Objectives (Goals)

With the understanding that a purpose for communicating is essential, identifying precisely what the purpose is in each instance becomes crucial even before specifics of instruction have been defined. This is often called "backward design." Backward design means in the context of classroom lesson planning that first desired outcomes, goals, or objectives are defined and then lessons are mapped out with the end in mind, the end being what students will be able to do after sufficient instruction and practice. Having well-crafted objectives or goals provides the standard by which learners' performance can be assessed or self-assessed.

World English lessons are designed on two-page spreads so students can easily see what is expected and what the context is. The goal that directly relates to the final application activity is identified at the beginning. Students, as well as instructors, can easily evaluate their performance as they attempt the final activity. Students can also readily see what tools they will practice to prepare them for the application activity. The application activity is a task where students can demonstrate their ability to perform what the lesson goal requires. This information provides direction and purpose for the learner. Students, who know what is expected, where they are going, and how they will get there, are more apt to reach success. Each success builds confidence and additional communication skills.

Tools and Skills

Once the lesson objective has been identified and a context established, the lesson developer must choose the tools the learner will need to successfully perform the task or objective. The developer can choose among various areas in communication building including vocabulary, grammar and pronunciation. The developer must also choose skills and strategies including reading, writing, listening, and speaking. The receptive skills of reading and listening are essential components to communication. All of these tools and skills must be placed in a balanced way into a context providing practice that can be transferred to their final application or learner demonstration which ultimately becomes evidence of communication building.

World English units are divided into "lessons" that each consists of a two-page spread. Each spread focuses on different skills and strategies and is labeled by a letter (A-E). The units contain the following lesson sequence:

- A: Vocabulary
- B: Listening and Pronunciation
- C: Language Expansion
- D: Reading/Writing
- E: Video Journal

Additional grammar and vocabulary are introduced as tools throughout to provide practice for the final application activity. Each activity in a page spread has the purpose of developing adequate skills to perform the final application task.

LAST WORD

The philosophy of World English is to provide motivating context to connect students to the world through which they build communication skills. These skills are developed, practiced, and assessed from lesson to lesson through initially identifying the objective and giving learners the tools they need to complete a final application task. The concept of performance is highlighted over merely learning new information and performance comes from communicating about meaningful and useful context. An accumulation of small communication skills leads to true and effective communication outside of the classroom in real-world environments.

	Unit Goals	Grammar	Vocabulary
UNIT 1 Friends and Family Page 2	• Meet and introduce people • Identify family members • Describe people • Present your family	Present tense *be* *I'm Kim.* *They're Maria and Lola.* *Be* + adjective *They're young. Is John single?* Questions with *be* and short answers *Are you married? Yes, I am/ No I'm not.*	Greetings and introductions Family members Adjectives to describe people
UNIT 2 Jobs Around the World Page 14	• Identify jobs • Talk about jobs • Talk about countries • Compare jobs in different countries	Contractions with *be:* (negative); Indefinite articles *He isn't a doctor. Pat's an artist.* *Be* + article + adjective + noun *Russia is a big country.*	Jobs Numbers Words to describe the weather Continents, countries, and cities
UNIT 3 Houses and Apartments Page 26	• Identify places in a home • Describe your house • Identify household objects • Compare houses	*There is/There are* *There are three bedrooms.* *Is there a garage?* Prepositions of place: *in, on, under, next to* *Your magazine is under your bag.*	Places in a home Furniture and household objects

TEDTALKS Video Page 38 **Kent Larson: Brilliant Designs to Fit More People in Every City** Video Strategy: Using Visual Cues

	Unit Goals	Grammar	Vocabulary
UNIT 4 Possessions Page 42	• Identify personal possessions • Talk about other people's possessions • Buy a present • Talk about special possessions	Demonstrative adjectives *Are these your books? That is not your bag.* Possessive nouns *It's Jim's bag.* *Have* *She has a camcorder.*	Personal possessions Electronic products
UNIT 5 Daily Activities Page 54	• Tell time • Talk about people's daily activities • Talk about what you do at work or school • Describe a dream job	Simple present tense: statements, negatives, *What time...?* questions, and short answers *They get up at 7 o'clock. What time do you start work?* Adverbs of frequency: *always, sometimes, never* *I never answer the phone.* Time expressions	Daily activities Telling time Work and school activities Time expressions
UNIT 6 Getting There Page 66	• Ask for and give directions • Create and use a tour route • Describe transportation • Record a journey	Prepositions of Place; Imperatives *Turn left and walk for two blocks. The hotel is across from the park.* *Have to* *She has to change buses.*	City landmarks Directions Ground transportation

TEDTALKS Video Page 78 **Karen Bass: Unseen Footage, Untamed Nature**

Listening	Speaking and Pronunciation	Reading	Writing	Video Journal
Listening for general understanding and specific information People describing their families	Talking about your family The /r/ sound	**National Geographic:** "Families around the World"	Writing sentences to describe your family	**National Geographic:** "Animal Families"
Focused listening People describing their jobs	Asking for and giving personal information Numbers Contractions with *be*	**National Geographic:** "Different Farmers"	Writing a paragraph to describe a person's job	**National Geographic:** "A Job for Children"
Listening for general understanding and specific details People talking about their houses	Describing your house Final *−s*	**TED**TALKS "Kent Larson: Brilliant Designs to Fit More People in Every City"	Writing descriptions of houses Writing Strategy: Topic Sentence	**National Geographic:** "A Very Special Village"
Listening for specific information People proving ownership	Talking about the personal possessions of others /i/ and /ɪ/ sounds	**National Geographic:** "Jewelry"	Summarizing a class survey Using commas	**National Geographic:** "Uncovering the Past"
Listening for general understanding and specific details Describing a photographer's work	Asking and answering questions about work or school activities Falling intonation on statements and information questions	**TED**TALKS "Karen Bass: Unseen Footage, Untamed Nature"	Writing a job description	**National Geographic:** "Zoo Dentists"
Listening for specific information Radio ad for a tour	Ask for and give directions *Yes/No* questions and short answers	**National Geographic:** "Journey to Antarctica"	Writing a travel itinerary	**National Geographic:** "Volcano Trek"

	Unit Goals	Grammar	Vocabulary
UNIT 7 **Free Time** Page 82	• Identify activities that are happening now • Make a phone call • Talk about abilities • Talk about sports	Present continuous tense *I'm not watching* TV. *I'm reading.* *Can* for ability He **can't** play the guitar. He **can** sing.	Pastimes Games and sports
UNIT 8 **Clothes** Page 94	• Identify and shop for clothes • Buy clothes • Express likes and dislikes • Learn about clothes and colors	*Can/Could* (for polite requests) **Can** I try on these shoes? Likes and dislikes I **love** your sweater! She **hates** pink.	Colors Clothes
UNIT 9 **Eat Well** Page 106	• Order a meal • Plan a party • Describe your diet • Talk about a healthy diet	*Some and any* There's **some** ice cream in the fridge. *How much/How many* **How many** oranges do we need? **How much** chocolate do we have?	Food types Meals Quantities Count/non-count nouns

TEDTALKS **Video** Page 118 **Ron Finley: A Guerilla Gardener in South Central L.A.** Video Strategy: Using Visual Cues

	Unit Goals	Grammar	Vocabulary
UNIT 10 **Health** Page 122	• Identify parts of the body to say how you feel • Ask about and describe symptoms • Identify remedies and give advice • Describe how to prevent health problems	Review of simple present tense My back **hurts**. *Look* + adjective *Feel* + adjective John **looks** terrible. I **feel** sick. *Should* (for advice) You **should** take an aspirin.	Parts of the body Common illnesses Remedies
UNIT 11 **Making Plans** Page 134	• Plan special days • Describe holiday traditions • Make life plans • Express wishes and plans	*Be going to* What **are** you **going to** do? We **are going to** have a party. *Would like to* for wishes I **would like to** be a doctor.	Special plans American holidays Professions
UNIT 12 **On the Move** Page 146	• Use the simple past • Give biographical information • Describe a move • Discuss migrations	Simple past tense We **went** to the mountains. He **moved** from San Francisco to New York.	Verbs + prepositions of movement Preparing to move

TEDTALKS **Video** Page 158 **Derek Sivers: Weird or Different?**

Listening	Speaking and Pronunciation	Reading	Writing	Video Journal
Listening for specific information Telephone conversation	Have a phone conversation /ʃ/ and /tʃ/ sounds *Can* and *can't*	**National Geographic:** "Soccer—The Beautiful Game"	Writing sentences about your abilities	**National Geographic:** "Danny's Challenge"
Listening for specific details Listening to people shopping for clothes	Describing people's clothes *Could you*	**National Geographic:** "Chameleon Clothes"	Writing about what people are wearing	**National Geographic:** "Traditional Silk-Making"
Listening for specific details Conversation to confirm a shopping list	Planning a dinner *And*	**TED**TALKS "Ron Finley: A Guerilla Gardener in South Central L.A."	Writing sentences about eating habits Writing Strategy: Self-Correct	**National Geographic:** "Slow Food"
Listening for general understanding and specific details Describing symptoms to a doctor	Describing symptoms and illnesses; giving advice Sentence stress	**National Geographic:** "Preventing Disease"	Writing a paragraph on disease prevention	**National Geographic:** "Farley, the Red Panda"
Listening for general understanding and specific details American holiday traditions	Talking about celebrating holidays *Be going to* (reduced form)	**TED**TALKS "Derek Sivers: Keep Your Goals to Yourself"	Writing about one's plans for the future	**National Geographic:** "Making a Thai Boxing Champion"
Listening for general understanding and specific details Biographies of famous immigrants	Discussing moving *-ed* endings	**National Geographic:** "Human Migration"	Writing a vacation postcard	**National Geographic:** "Monarch Migration"

Friends and Family

Around the world, people have friends and family that come from many different age groups and backgrounds.

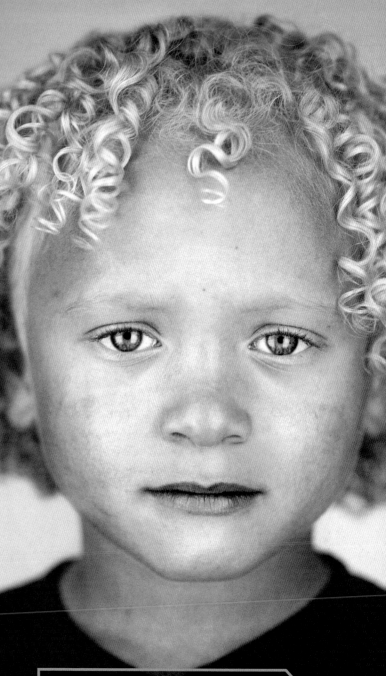

UNIT 1 GOALS

1. Meet and introduce people

2. Identify family members

3. Describe people

4. Present your family

3

Vocabulary

A 🔊 2 Listen and repeat.

Greetings

Informal

Hi! How's it going?

Great! And you?

Fine.
OK.
So-so.

Formal

Good morning. How are you?

Fine, thank you. And how are you?

Good afternoon.
Good evening.

B 👥 Greet your classmates informally.

C Greet your teacher formally.

D 🔊 3 Listen and repeat.

Introductions

Formal

(Hello.) Pleased to meet you. My name's Alan.

Hi. I'm Elsa.

Informal

This is my friend Hussein.

Nice to meet you, Hussein.

Nice to meet you, too.

Word Focus

🔊 4 The English alphabet =
A B C D E F G H I J K L M N O
P Q R S T U V W X Y Z

Real Language

We sometimes spell our names for people.

—**How do you spell that?**
—**Sam: S-A-M.**

E 👥 Introduce yourself to your classmates. Spell your name for them.

F 🔄 Role-play with a partner. One of you is the teacher. One of you is the student. Introduce yourself formally to your teacher. Use your last name.

G 👥 Work in groups of three. Practice introducing each other.

Grammar: Present tense *be*

Subject pronoun	Be	
I	**am**	
You	**are**	Kim.
He/She	**is**	
We	**are**	Lucas and Ed.
They	**are**	Maria and Claudia.

Contractions with *be*
I**'m**
you**'re**
he**'s**/she**'s**
we**'re**
they**'re**

Possessive adjectives	
My	name is Mario.
Your	name is Rachel.
His	name is Robert.
Her	name is Liujun.
Their	names are Ben and Dan.

A Write the correct form of the verb *be*.

1. Their names ___are___ Julie and Les.
2. My name ___is___ Irwin.
3. I ___am___ Said.
4. We ___are___ Rigo and Rosana.
5. His name ___is___ Arata.
6. Your name ___is___ Yan-Ching.

B Unscramble the sentences.

1. Ron. name My is   My name is Ron.
2. Leila. is name Her   name is Leila.
3. is name Mr. Aoki. His   name is Mr. Aoki
4. Tim. Their Jan names are and   Their name is Jan and Tim.

C Write the sentences again. Use contractions.

1. He is Ruben.   He's Ruben.
2. I am Diego.   I'm Diego
3. You are Rebecca.   You're Rebecca
4. They are Ashley and Hana.   They're Ashley and Hana

Real Language

When we introduce ourselves formally, we sometimes use our last name as well.

Hello. My name's Peter <u>Derby</u>.

Conversation

A 🔊 5 Listen to the conversation.

Donna: Hi, Nick. How are you?
Nick: Great. And you?
Donna: Fine.

Nick: Donna, this is my friend Hiroshi.
Donna: Nice to meet you, Hir . . . sorry?
Hiroshi: It's Hiroshi. H-I-R-O-S-H-I. Nice to meet you, Donna.

B 👥 Practice the conversation in groups of three.

C 👥 Practice the conversation again. Use your own names.

D 🔄 **GOAL CHECK** ✔ **Meet and introduce people**

Work in pairs. Find another pair and introduce each other.

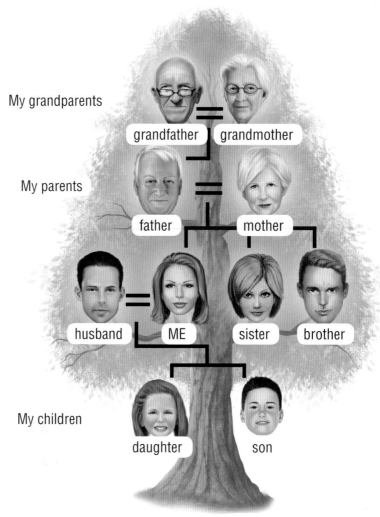

My grandparents — grandfather grandmother

My parents — father mother

husband ME sister brother

My children — daughter son

Listening

A 🔊 6 Listen to Carlos introduce his family. Point to the people and pets.

B 🔊 6 Listen again. Circle **T** for *true* and **F** for *false*.

Carlos says:

1. This is my grandfather. His name is Pedro. (T) F
2. This is my sister. Her name is Karina. (T) F
3. This is my grandmother. Her name is Elena. T (F)
4. This is my father. His name is Jose Manuel. T (F)
5. These are our dogs. Their names are Lucy and Lulu. (T) F

C Correct any *false* sentences. Take turns to read all the sentences to a partner.

D Fill in the blanks in Carlos's family tree.

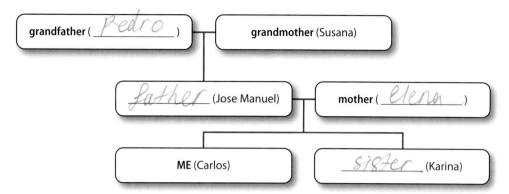

grandfather (_Pedro_)

grandmother (Susana)

father (Jose Manuel)

mother (_Elena_)

ME (Carlos)

sister (Karina)

E Complete the sentences.

1. Karina is Jose Manuel's _daughter_ .
2. Jose Manuel is Elena's _husband_ .
3. Susana and Pedro are Carlos's _grandparents_ .
4. Karina is Carlos's _sister_ .
5. Karina's parents are _father_ and _mother_ .

Pronunciation: The /r/ sound

A 🔊 7 <u>Underline</u> the letter *r*. Listen to the /r/ sound and repeat the word.

| father | sister | Rick | Robert Brown |
| mother | brother | Rose | Mary Brown |

B Take turns reading the words to a partner.

Communication

A Draw your own family tree.

B Describe your family tree to a partner.

C **GOAL CHECK** ✔ **Identify family members**

Bring some family photos to class. Introduce your family to your classmates.

This is my grandmother. Her name is Aiko.

Language Expansion: Adjectives

He is tall with short black hair.

▲ curly black hair

▲ straight gray hair ▲ wavy red hair

▲ straight blond hair ▲ curly brown hair

▲ short tall   ▲ old young   ▲ married single   ▲ attractive

A Now describe yourself.

I am ___*tall*___ with ___*short + Black*___ hair.

B 🔁 With a partner, take turns to describe yourself. Then describe your classmates. Use the verb *be* with adjectives and the word *with* to describe hair.

I am young with straight black hair.

David is tall with curly black hair.

C Describe a student to the class. The class guesses who you are describing.

Grammar: *Be* + adjective

Subject + *be* + adjective					
I	**am**	young.	Emily	**is**	young and short.
You	**are**	tall and handsome.	We	**are**	married.
John	**is**	old with gray hair.	They	**are**	tall with black curly hair.

Questions with *be* and short answers

Questions			Short answers	
Are	you	married?	Yes, I **am**.	No, I**'m not**.
Is	he/she	single?	Yes, he/she **is**.	No, he/she **isn't**. No, he**'s**/she**'s not**.
Are	they	married?	Yes, they **are**.	No, they**'re not**. No, they **aren't**.

Real Language

When we want to call someone *attractive*, we usually say *handsome* for a man, and *pretty* for a woman.

A Match the questions and the answers.

Questions

1. Is your brother tall? _b_
2. Are your brothers married? _c_ .
3. Is Emma tall? _a_
4. Is your brother single? _e_
5. Are your mother and father old? _d_ .

Answers

a. Yes, she is.
b. No, he isn't. He's short.
c. Chen is married. Lee isn't.
d. No, they're not.
e. No, he isn't. He's married.

B Fill in the blanks with a question or an answer.

1. **Q:** Is she short ?
   A: No, she isn't. She's tall.
2. **Q:** Is she tall with Black hair ?
   A: No, she isn't. She is short with blond hair.
3. **Q:** Is Alicia attractive?
   A: Yes, she is.
4. **Q:** Is she married ?
   A: Yes, she is. Her husband's name is Marco.

Conversation

A 🔊 8 Listen to the conversation.

Ana: Who's this in the photo?
Carol: It's my <u>brother</u>.
Ana: What's <u>his</u> name?
Carol: <u>Richard</u>.

Ana: Is <u>he</u> married?
Carol: Yes, <u>he</u> is.
Ana: Too bad!

B 🔁 Practice the conversation with a partner. Switch roles and practice it again.

C 🔁 Change the underlined words and make a new conversation.

D 🔁 Take turns asking your partner questions about himself/herself. Then, introduce your partner to the class.

> This is Salma. That's S-A-L-M-A. She is young with curly brown hair.

E 🔁 **GOAL CHECK** ✔ **Describe people**

Describe three people to your partner. They can be people you know or celebrities.

Reading

A Look at the pictures. Guess the family relations.

> **This man is married to this woman.**

Now read and check your guesses.

B Complete the sentences with the words from the box.

> mother long son
> five pretty black

1. Rose is the ___mother___ of Bao.
2. Minh has ___short black___ hair.
3. Trang and Thuy are ___older than their brothers___.
4. Bachau and Mishri have ___five___ children.
5. Guddi and Aarti have ___long___ hair.
6. Anil is the ___son___ of Bachau.

C Circle the correct answers.

1. Her father is Anh Hoang.
   a. Thuy   **b.** Seema

2. His wife is Mishri.
   a. Anh   **b.** Bachau

3. Her brother is Bao.
   a. Trang   **b.** Guddi

4. Guddu is the brother of
   a. Minh   **b.** Anil

5. Their mother is Rose.
   a. Thuy and Bao   **b.** Guddi and Aarti

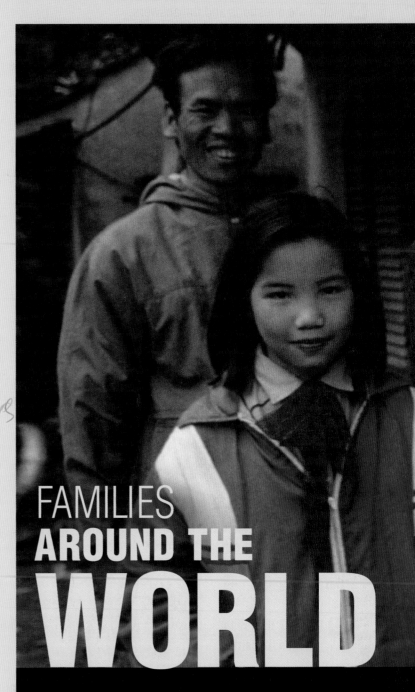

FAMILIES AROUND THE WORLD

This is the Hoang family. Let's start with the parents, Anh and Rose Hoang. They are married and have two sons and their names are Minh and Bao. Minh has short black hair. Bao's hair is a little longer. Anh's hair is longer than Minh's or Bao's. Anh and Rose have two daughters. Their names are Trang and Thuy. They are older than their brothers. They are both pretty and wear colorful clothing.

This is the Yadav family. Bachau and Mishri Yadav are married and they have five children. They have three girls: Guddi, Seema, and Aarti, and two boys: Guddu and Anil. Guddi and Aarti have long hair. The rest of the family has shorter hair. They spend a lot of time together. They are a happy family.

Communication

 Look at the pictures. Choose one picture. Describe that person to a partner. Your partner guesses who you are describing.

Martin Schoeller is famous for taking close-up photos. His subjects include famous people, twins, and the changing face of America. These are some of his photos.

> She is tall with curly hair. She is young.

> Is it Marta?

> Yes, it is!

1. Marta

2. Daisy

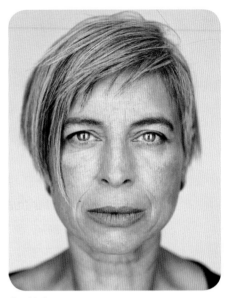

4. Helen

3. Mars

Writing

A Show your family portrait to your partner and describe your family.

> This is my father. His name is Salim. He is handsome with short black hair.

B Choose three members of your family and write a description of them.

C **GOAL CHECK** ✔ **Present your family**

Work with a partner. Take turns describing your family.

1. _____

2. _____

3. _____

Before You Watch

A Label the animals. Use the words in the box.

| female lion   leopard |
| male gorilla   meerkats |
| polar bears |

While You Watch

A ▶ Watch the video. Circle **T** for *true* and **F** for *false*.

1. Polar bears have big families.   T   F
2. Lions live in family groups.   (T)   F
3. Meerkats are big.   T   (F)
4. Female gorillas have gray (silver) hair on their backs.   T   (F)

4. _____

B ▶ Complete the sentences. Use the words in the box. Then watch the video again to check your answers.

| pretty   big   long   male |

1. A male lion has _Long_ hair on his neck.
2. Meerkats live in _big_ groups.
3. Young meerkats are _____.
4. The _male_ gorilla is the leader of the family.

5. _____

After You Watch

A 🗘 What animals do you know that fit in these categories? With a partner, fill in the chart, then share your answers with the class.

	Big	Small
Live in groups	lions	bees
Live alone	polar bears	

Jobs Around the World

Workers paint a 140-meter-high tower at a factory in Huaibei, China.

Look at the photo, answer the questions:

1 Where are these people from?   **2** What is their job?

UNIT 2 GOALS

1. Identify jobs

2. Talk about jobs

3. Talk about countries

4. Compare jobs in different countries

15

taxi driver	chef	teacher
engineer	artist	doctor
architect	banker	

Vocabulary

A 🔊 **9** What do they do? Listen and label the pictures with words from the box.

1. Oscar: _teacher_

2. Eun: _artist_

3. Jane: _engineer_

4. Dae-Jung: _chef_

5. Jim: _taxi driver_

6. Hannah: _doctor_

7. Harvey: _banker_

8. Fernanda: _architect_

B In your opinion, are these jobs interesting or boring? Write the jobs from exercise **A** on the lines.

banker taxi driver artist doctor engineer Teacher chef architect

boring ←————————————————————————————————————→ interesting

C 🔄 Compare your answers with a partner's answers.

Grammar: Contractions with *be* (negative); Indefinite articles

Contractions			Indefinite articles
I'm **not**			**a** chef.
You**'re not**		You **aren't**	**an** artist.
He**'s**/She**'s not**	OR	He/She **isn't**	
We**'re**/They**'re not**		We/They **aren't**	artists.
			*We use **a** before a consonant sound. *We use **an** before a vowel sound.

A Look at the pictures on the opposite page. Fill in the blanks with *is* or *is not*.

1. Jim _____is_____ a taxi driver. He ____is not____ a doctor.
2. Oscar ____is____ a teacher. He ___is not___ an architect.
3. Fernanda ____is____ an architect. She ___is not___ a doctor.
4. Dae-Jung ___is not___ an engineer. He ____is____ a chef.
5. Eun ___is not___ a banker. He ____is____ an artist.

B Fill in the blanks with *a* or *an*. Then circle **T** for *true* and **F** for *false*.

1. Hannah is __a__ taxi driver.   T   (F)
2. Jane is __an__ engineer.   (T) F
3. Dae-Jung is __an__ artist.   T   (F)
4. Eun is not __a__ doctor.   (T) (F)
5. Harvey is not __an__ architect.   T   (F)

▲ This is Aran. Describe him. What is his job?

C ⟳ Correct the false sentences in your notebook. Read the new sentences to a partner.

Conversation

A 🔊 **10** Listen to the conversation. Is Jill married or single?

Mary: Hi, Jean. How's life?
Jean: Fine. And you?
Mary: Great. How are the children?
Jean: They're good. But they're not children now. Jim's married. He's <u>an engineer</u>.
Mary: <u>Wow</u>! Time passes. And what about Jill? How old is she now?
Jean: She's <u>21</u> and she's <u>a student</u>.
Mary: Is she married?
Jean: No, she's single.

B ⟳ Practice the conversation with a partner. Switch roles and practice it again.

C ⟳ Change the underlined words and make a new conversation.

D ⚙ **GOAL CHECK** ✔ **Identify jobs**

Ask your classmates about their jobs. Ask them about the jobs of people in their families.

Real Language

To show surprise, we can say:
formal ⟵⟶ informal
Really!   Amazing!   Wow!

What do you do?

What does your father do?

▲ Michelle

▲ Carlos

▲ Salim

Listening

A 🔊 11 Look at the pictures. Guess each person's age and job. Listen and check your guesses.

B 🔊 11 Listen again. Fill in the blanks in the chart.

	Michelle	Carlos	Salim
How old is he/she?	28	45	44
What is his/her job?	a. opt'k	Taxi	officer
Is his/her job interesting?	love yes	not very	yes

C 🔄 Work with a partner. Take turns reading the numbers in English.

Numbers	**10** ten	**20** twenty	**30** thirty
1 one	**11** eleven	**21** twenty-one	**40** forty
2 two	**12** twelve	**22** twenty-two	**50** fifty
3 three	**13** thirteen	**23** twenty-three	**60** sixty
4 four	**14** fourteen	**24** twenty-four	**70** seventy
5 five	**15** fifteen	**25** twenty-five	**80** eighty
6 six	**16** sixteen	**26** twenty-six	**90** ninety
7 seven	**17** seventeen	**27** twenty-seven	**100** one hundred
8 eight	**18** eighteen	**28** twenty-eight	**101** one hundred
9 nine	**19** nineteen	**29** twenty-nine	and one

D 👥 Take a survey of your classmates. Ask these questions:

1. What is your name?

2. How old are you?

3. How old are your parents?

4. How old are your grandparents?

Pronunciation: Numbers

A 🔊 12 Listen and circle what you hear.

1. six   sixteen   sixty
2. four   fourteen   forty
3. three   thirteen   thirty

4. seven   seventeen   seventy
5. eight   (eighteen)   eighty

B 🔊 13 Listen and write the numbers.

1. I have _____8_____ brothers and _____2_____ sisters.
2. Alan is _____16_____ and his grandfather is _____60_____.
3. We have _____9_____ children. Bae is _____15_____,
   Chin Ho is _____11_____, and Dong-Min is _____5_____.
4. There are _____24_____ students in the class.
   4

C 🔄 Work with a partner. Take turns reading the sentences in **B**.

Pronunciation: Contractions with *be*

▲ He's a photographer. Is his job interesting?

A 🔊 14 Listen and circle what you hear.

1. **A:** Is Fatima an artist?
   B: (No,) (she isn't | she's not) an artist. (She's | She is) a doctor.

2. **A:** Are Bill and Jane married?
   B: No, (they aren't | they're not) married. (They're | They are) single.

3. **A:** Look! A leopard!
   B: (It's | It is) a lion. (It isn't | It's not) a leopard.

4. **A:** Are they teachers?
   B: No, (they aren't | they're not). (They're | They are) students!

B 🔄 Listen again. Take turns practicing the conversations in **A** with a partner.

Communication

A 👥 Read the questions and answer them for yourself. Use a dictionary if you need to. Then ask two classmates the questions. Write their answers.

Questions	Me	Classmate 1	Classmate 2
What is your name?			
How old are you?			
What is your job?			
Is it interesting?			

B 🔄 **GOAL CHECK** ✓ **Talk about jobs**

Tell a partner about the people you interviewed.

> Ivan is 27 years old and he's a chef.

> His job is interesting.

▲ wet

▲ hot

▲ cold

▲ dry

Language Expansion: Countries and cities

A Guess the country.

1. It's in Asia. It's big. The capital is Beijing. _China_

2. It's in Europe. It's small. It's wet. _England_

3. It's in South America. It's big. It's hot. _Br_

4. It's in South America. The capital is Santiago. _Chile_

5. It's in North America. It's hot. _____

6. It's in Europe and Asia. It's a very big country and it's very cold. _Russia_

7. It's in Asia. It's hot. The capital is New Delhi. _India_

8. It's in Africa. It is hot and dry. _____

Grammar: *Be* + adjective + noun

Statement	Question	Answer
Africa **is** a big continent.	**Is** the United Kingdom (UK) a big country?	No, it **isn't**. It's a small country.
Egypt **is** a hot, dry country.	**Is** the United States a big country?	Yes, it **is**.

▲ Cairo is the capital of Egypt.

A Unscramble the sentences and questions.

1. China Is a country? big   *Is ...*
2. big The is a country. United States   *Yes, it is*
3. is a Russia country. cold   *Yes, it is, it's big.*
4. Is hot Egypt a country?   *Yes, it is hot country*
5. country? small Japan Is a   *Is Japan small country?*

B Answer the questions.

1. Is Mexico a cold country?   No, it isn't. It's a hot country.
2. Is Chile a big country?   *No, it isn't. It's a small country.*
3. Is Japan a hot country?   *Yes, it is. It's a hot country*
4. Is the UK a small country?   *No, it isn't. It's a big country*
5. Is Egypt a wet country?   *No, it isn't. It's a hot, dry country*

Conversation

A 🔊 **15** Listen to the conversation. Where is Mohamed from?

Chris: Where do you come from, <u>Mohamed</u>?
Mohamed: I'm from <u>Cairo</u>.
Chris: <u>Cairo</u> is in <u>Egypt</u>, right?
Mohamed: Yes.

Chris: So, tell me about <u>Egypt, Mohamed</u>.
Mohamed: Well, it's in <u>Africa—North Africa</u>.
Chris: Is it a <u>hot</u> country?
Mohamed: Yes, it's <u>very hot</u>.

B 🔁 Practice the conversation with a partner. Switch roles and practice it again.

C 🔁 Change the underlined words and make a new conversation.

D 🔁 **GOAL CHECK** ✔ **Talk about countries**

Talk to a partner. Choose a country. Write a description of the country. Read it to the class. The class has to guess the country.

Reading

A Look at the pictures. These people are farmers. Where do you think they come from?

B Read and complete the sentences.

1. Sofia and Yaroslaw are from
   Poland.

2. They are ___have a big farm__.

3. Their potatoes go to countries like
   for family and
   Germany and England

4. Jose is from _Yucatan_.

5. He grows ___beans___ and
   ___maize___.

6. He is ___married___ with
   three ___children___.

C Answer the questions.

1. Do Sofia and Yaroslaw come from Peru?
   No it isn't   it is a Poland

2. Is it hot in Poland in the summer?
   No, it isn't, it is cool and wet

3. Is their farm big?
   Yes, it is

4. Is Jose married?
   yes, when ma she is

5. Is he a potato farmer?
   No, it isn't

6. Is it hot in Mexico in the summer?
   . Yes, it is

DIFFERENT FARMERS

Sofia is from Poland and she and her husband, Yaroslaw, are potato farmers. They have a big farm of about 55 hectares. The weather in Poland is good for potatoes because it is cool and wet in the summer. People in Poland eat a lot of potatoes. Some of the potatoes are for their family but they sell some of their potatoes to other countries, like Germany and England.

Jose is also a farmer and he comes from Yucatan in Mexico. He is twenty-four years old and he is married with three small children. He is not a potato farmer. He is a maize farmer, and he also grows beans. The summer in Mexico is very hot and wet, and this is good for maize and beans. His wife makes *tortillas* from the maize and their children love tortillas with beans.

▲ Aapti

▲ Henry

Aapti is from Nepal. She
is a farmer, but her farm
is very small. She grows
rice. Her rice does not go
to other countries. It is for
her family.

Communication

A In your notebook, make a list of jobs you know.

B Compare your list with a partner. Name three jobs that are interesting. Name three jobs that are boring.

C Look at the pictures. Discuss the following questions with a partner.

1. Where do you think these people are from?

2. What do they do?

3. Are they old or young?

4. Are their jobs interesting?

Writing

A Read about Aapti. Write a similar paragraph about Henry. Use these words: United States, big, wheat, Asia.

She is Rice, does for family.
Nepal is in t a a big contry in
she is farm very big

B GOAL CHECK ✓ **Compare jobs in different countries**

Talk to a partner about farmers in your country. What do they grow? What is the weather like? Are their jobs interesting or boring?

sky

cliffs

sea

beach

box

a puffin

Before You Watch

A 🔄 Work with a partner. Look at the pictures. Answer these questions.

1. What do these children do?   2. Is their job interesting?

While You Watch

A ▶ Watch the video. Circle **T** for *true* and **F** for *false*.

1. Puffin patrols look for bird nests. T **(F)**
2. There are puffin nests in the cliffs. **(T)** F
3. All the puffins fly out to sea. T **(F)**
4. Some puffins get lost in town. **(T)** F
5. Puffin patrols rescue pufflings. **(T)** F

B ▶ Complete the sentences with the words or phrases in the box. Watch the video again to check your answers.

| look for   leave   throw   get lost |

1. Some puffins ___get lost___ in town.
2. The pufflings ___leave___ the cliffs.
3. The children ___throw___ the pufflings out to sea.
4. The puffin patrols ___look for___ the lost pufflings in parking lots.

After You Watch

A 🔄 Work with a partner. Take turns describing the job of the puffin patrols.

light

town

buildings

pier

parking lot

flashlight

street

▲ A puffin patrol looks for and rescues lost pufflings.

Houses and Apartments

The "fronds" of the $14-billion Palm Jumeirah—
the first of three planned resort islands in Dubai,
United Arab Emirates—jut into the Persian Gulf.

UNIT 3 GOALS

1. Identify places in a home

2. Describe your house

3. Identify household objects

4. Compare houses

Vocabulary

A Label the rooms in the floor plan of the apartment.

B Complete the sentences about the house in the picture. Use the words in the box.

| garage   downstairs   swimming pool   bedroom |

1. The kitchen is ___downstairs___.
2. The ___swimming___ is in the backyard.
3. The ___bedroom___ is upstairs.
4. The car is in the ___garage___.

Grammar: *There is/There are*

Statement	Questions	Answers
There is a garage.	**Is there** a closet?	Yes, **there is.** No, **there isn't.**
There are three bedrooms upstairs.	**Are there** two bathrooms?	Yes, **there are.** No, **there aren't.**

*The contraction of *there is* = *there's*.

Singular nouns	Plural nouns
1 house 1 bedroom	2 houses 2 bedrooms

*Add an -s at the end of the word to make it plural.

A Complete the sentences with the correct form: *there is* or *there are*.

1. _there is_ a big kitchen.
2. _there are_ three bathrooms.
3. _Is there_ a yard?
4. Are there stairs? Yes, _there are_.
5. Is there a garage? No, _there aren't_.

B Unscramble the sentences and questions.

1. a is big There garage.
2. isn't There closet. a
3. a swimming Is there pool?
4. there two Are bathrooms?
5. bedrooms. are There two

Is there a big garage?
isn't there not a closet?
Is there a swimming pool?
Are there two bathrooms?
Are there two bedrooms?

C Write questions to ask about somebody's house. Use these words.

1. bathroom/upstairs
   Is there a bathroom upstairs?

2. swimming pool/backyard
   Is there a swimming pool?

3. stairs/your house
   Is there a your house

4. garden/front yard
   Is there a front and yard garde

5. three bedrooms/your house
   Are there a bedrooms and your house

6. closet/bedroom
   Is there

D 🔁 Ask your partner the questions in exercise **C**. Switch roles.

Conversation

A 🔊 16 Listen to the conversation. Is there a garage?

Realtor: What about this <u>apartment</u>?
Client: Is it a big <u>apartment</u>?
Realtor: Yes. There <u>are three bedrooms</u>.
Client: And bathrooms?

Realtor: There is just one bathroom.
Client: Is there a <u>garden</u>?
Realtor: No, there isn't. But there's a <u>garage</u>.

B 🔁 Practice the conversation with a partner. Switch roles and practice it again.

C 🔁 Change the underlined words and make a new conversation.

D 🔁 **GOAL CHECK** ✔ **Identify places in a home**

Work with a partner. Draw a floor plan of your own home. Tell your partner about your home.

Listening

A 🔊 **17** Guess how many bedrooms there are in these houses. Listen and check your guess. Then write the person's name for each house.

1. _____Joe's_____

2. _____Heidi's_____
two bedROOMS

3. _____Li's home_____

4. _____Ali's home_____

B 🔊 **17** Listen again. Match the house and the description.

1. Heidi's home _____   a. big, no garden
2. Joe's home _____   b. not big, one bedroom
3. Ali's home _____   c. big, garden
4. Li's home _____   d. not big, two bedrooms

C 🔊 **17** Listen again. Circle **T** for *true* and **F** for *false*.

1. It is cold in Heidi's house.   T   **F**
2. There are three bathrooms in Joe's house. **T**   F
3. There is a dining room in Li's apartment. T   **F**
4. There are six bedrooms in Ali's house.   T   **F**

Pronunciation: Final -s

A 🔊 **18** Listen and check the correct column.

	Ends in /s/ sound	Ends in /z/ sound	Ends in /iz/ sound
gardens	✓		
apartments	✓		
garages			✓
bathrooms		✓	
kitchens		✓	
houses			✓
closets	✓		

B 🔊 **18** Listen again and repeat the words.

Communication

A 🔄 Work with a partner. Take turns describing these houses. Use your imagination.

> **There is one bedroom in this house.**

B 👥 | **GOAL CHECK** ✓ **Describe your house**

Describe your house to the class.

Language Expansion: Furniture and household objects

▲ chair   ▲ armchair   ▲ table   ▲ microwave

▲ stove   ▲ bookcase   ▲ coffee table   ▲ lamp   ▲ refrigerator

▲ TV   ▲ sofa   ▲ bed

A In which rooms do you usually find the furniture and household objects above?

Kitchen	Dining room	Living room	Bedroom
stove Refrigerator table microwave chair	table armchair	TV sofa coffeetable book case	bed Lamp

Grammar: Prepositions of place

A Where is the computer?

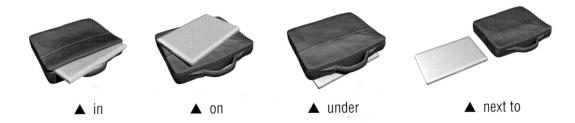

▲ in   ▲ on   ▲ under   ▲ next to

B Look at the pictures. Complete the sentences with *in, on, under,* or *next to*.

1. There's a TV _____*in*_____ the bedroom.
2. There's a boy _____*in*_____ the swimming pool.
3. There are four books _____*on*_____ the table.
4. The stove is _____*next to*_____ the refrigerator.
5. The dog is _____*under*_____ the table.

C What can you see in the pictures? Take turns describing them.

> There is a sofa and a coffee table.

Conversation

A ◀))) 19 Listen to the conversation. Where is Tracey's magazine?

Tracey: Where is my <u>magazine</u>?
Kevin: Is it in the <u>bedroom</u>?
Tracey: No, it isn't. And it's not on the <u>kitchen table</u>.
Kevin: Here it is! It's under your <u>bag</u>.

B Practice the conversation with a partner. Switch roles and practice it again.

C Change the underlined words and make a new conversation that is true for you.

D **GOAL CHECK** ✔ **Identify household objects**

Work with a partner. Take turns describing a room in your house.

GOAL 4: Compare Houses

Reading

A Look at the picture and read the caption on page 35. What do you know about urban sprawl? Mark each statement true or false. Write *T* or *F*.

1. Urban sprawl = more and more people in the same space. _____

2. Urban sprawl is a problem in countries like China. _____

3. People are moving to the **countryside** to find jobs. _____

4. Cities can fit more people only by growing larger in size. _____

B 🗣 Are there large cities in your country? With a partner, describe those cities. What is a typical home like there?

> **Hong Kong is a city with a lot of people.**

> **The apartments are very small!**

C Read the article. Correct the false information.

model: Kent Larson is an ~~engineer.~~ *architect*

1. Cities will need more ~~jobs.~~ *houses or apar*

2. Many people are moving to the ~~countryside.~~ *to siti is affordable*

3. Small apartments are **expensive,** but people don't like them.

4. Kent Larson designs a new type of house.

5. He uses furniture and design to solve a problem.

WORD BANK
affordable $
comfortable nice to live in
country(side) not a city
expensive $$$$
home where you live; a house or apartment
solve a problem fix something, make it better

Kent Larson Architect

BRILLIANT DESIGNS TO FIT MORE PEOPLE IN EVERY CITY

The following article is about Kent Larson. After Unit 3, you'll have the opportunity to watch some of Larson's TED Talk and learn more about his idea worth spreading.

This is Kent Larson. He is an architect. He wants to **solve a problem.** What problem? The world's population is growing, and more people are moving to cities. Where will all these people live?

These people all need houses or apartments. A city with many small apartments can fit more people than a city with large apartments or houses. Small apartments are **affordable** and use less energy. However, many people do not want to live in small **homes.** They want separate rooms in their homes for many different activities. This is a problem.

Kent Larson has an idea to solve this problem . . . a way to design homes in cities where people live **comfortably** in small spaces. He wants to use design and technology to make an entirely new type of apartment.

Urban sprawl can happen when many people move to a city in a short time.

"More than half (50+%) the people in the world now live in cities, and that will just continue to escalate (↗)."

– Kent Larson

There are 24 million people in Shanghai now. In 2020, there will be 26.5 million people living there.

Writing

A Look at this plan of a house. Complete the paragraph.

This is a plan of a house. There is a small kitchen. In the kitchen, there is a _stove_ and a refrigerator. The kitchen is next to the _dining_ room. In the dining room there is a table with eight chairs. The living room is _next to_ the dining room. There is a sofa and two armchairs in the living room. There are three _bedrooms_ in the house—one big bedroom and two small bedrooms.

B Read the Writing Strategy. Underline the topic sentence in the paragraph in exercise **A**.

C Draw a plan of your house. Then write a paragraph about your house. Underline the topic sentence.

Writing Strategy

A topic sentence tells the topic, or main idea, of a reading. It is usually near the beginning. Use a topic sentence to help your reader understand what you are writing about.

Communication

A In pairs, pick a growing city that you know. Which neighborhoods are traditional? Which neighborhoods are new?

B GOAL CHECK ✓ Compare houses

Work with a partner. Take turns comparing the homes in two of the neighborhoods you picked.

> There are houses with gardens in Coyoacán.

> Not in Santa Fe!

Before You Watch

A Complete the video summary. Use the words in the box.

fishermen   artists
village   paint   Sea   art

Video summary

Camogli is a small town, or _village_, in Italy. Camogli is next to the Mediterranean _Sea_.
Many people in Camogli are _artists_. Their job is to catch fish. There are also _artists_ in
Camogli. They _paint_ houses and buildings. Their _art_ is called *trompe l'oeil*. It is very
special. The paintings are very realistic. They make things look real, but they are not.

While You Watch

A ▶ Watch the video. Match the parts of the sentences.

1. Artists use *trompe l'oeil* to make _____   **a.** with bright colors.
2. People like to paint their houses _____   **b.** artists.
3. The fishermen painted their houses _____   **c.** things look real.
4. Raffaella and Carlo are _____   **d.** from the sea.
5. You can see the houses of Camogli _____   **e.** with *trompe l'oeil* art.

B ▶ Watch the video again. Circle **T** for *true* and **F** for *false*.

1. Camogli is a large city.   T   (F)
2. In Camogli, people paint their houses in bright colors.   (T)   F
3. The houses in Camogli are very special.   (T)   F
4. All the artists in Italy use the *trompe l'oeil* technique.   T   (F)
5. Only fishermen paint their houses with *trompe l'oeil* art.   T   (F)

After You Watch

A 🔄 Work with a partner. Take turns describing the changes you would make
to your house with *trompe l'oeil*.

> I want to add
> two balconies.

TEDTALKS

Kent Larson Architect
BRILLIANT DESIGNS TO FIT MORE PEOPLE IN EVERY CITY

Before You Watch

A Do you know what these words mean? Match each space (place) to its function (use).

Functions

guest dance exercise

work hang out, relax

Spaces

1. Office

_____WORK_____

2. Studio

_____dance_____.

3. Living room

_____

4. Gym

_____exircise_____.

5. Guest bedroom

_____guest_____

WORD FOCUS

A *studio* is also: a space for art; an apartment with only one room.

A *wall* separates one room from another room. For example, there is a wall between this classroom and the classroom next door.

Kent Larson's idea worth spreading is that cities are all about people, not cars, and their design should reflect that more clearly. Watch Larson's full TED Talk on TED.com.

B Match the word in **bold** to its meaning.

a. change

b. build, grow

c. move parts of something to make it bigger/smaller

d. go from one place to another

e. area

1. Janet **moves** from an apartment to a new house. _____

2. I **develop** my English skills in class. _____

3. There is **space** for four people in my car.

_____

4. **Fold** your paper and give it to a partner. **Unfold** the paper your partner gives you.

_____

5. In Rome, Americans **convert** their dollars ($) to euros (€). _____

C You are going to watch a TED Talk about a new way to design a house. Look at the pictures and the quotes on the next page. What do you think you will see?

1. A gym that converts into a dining room.

2. An apartment with walls that move.

3. A family that lives in a big space.

While You Watch

A Watch the video. Check what you see.

____ an architect ____ a bedroom

____ a kitchen ____ a dining room

____ an office ____ a garden

____ a doctor ____ a gym

____ a garage ____ a swimming pool

> "We can make a very small apartment that functions as if it's twice (2x) as big."
>
> – Kent Larson

There are not a lot of jobs in the countryside; most jobs are in the city. Families live in small apartments.

One architect, Kent Larson, has an idea for how to make a great home in a small space.

"The most interesting implementation (use)... is when you can begin to have robotic walls."

USING VISUAL CUES

Understanding every word is not important. Look at the images and the words in the video to help you understand the main idea. You can understand the main idea even when you don't know many of the words you hear.

In the next 15 years, 90% of population growth will be in cities.

After You Watch

A Watch the TED Talk again. Circle the word you hear.

1. Many cities do not have a lot of (space | home) for housing.

2. Your space can (develop | convert) from an exercise to a work place.

3. You have (guests | walls) over, you have two guest rooms that are developed.

4. You have a dinner party: the table (folds | converts) out to fit sixteen people.

5. I think you have to build dumb (studios | homes) and put smart stuff in them.

B Match the cause and effect, based on the video.

Cause

1. _____ There are not many jobs in the countryside. There are jobs in the cities.

2. _____ There is not a lot of space for housing in the cities.

3. _____ A wall moves.

4. _____ An engineer wants to exercise and work at home.

Effect

a. Families live in small spaces.

b. The space changes from a dining space to a guest bedroom

c. In his apartment, the gym converts into an office.

d. Families move to the cities.

C Correct the false information in each statement.

model: In the countryside, houses are often small. *big*

1. There are many jobs in the countryside.

2. Many people move to the cities to live in big houses.

3. In the city, many houses have a garden or backyard.

4. Kent Larson is a teacher.

5. In the apartment, the gym converts into a dining space.

6. To hang out, the walls unfold to make a kitchen.

7. The space to practice dance (or art, or music) is the guest bedroom.

8. This apartment is good in cities in places like Antarctica.

Project

Kent Larson wants to change the way we live in cities. Use his ideas to design a new home. Follow these steps.

A Interview your partner. Learn about his or her family and what types of spaces they need in their home. Ask these questions.

1. How many people do you live with?

2. Who are they?

3. How old are people?

4. Do you have family that visits? (grandparents, aunts, uncles)

5. What do they do when they visit? (stay a few days, come for dinner)

6. What do the people in your family do? Are they students, athletes, business people, etc?

B Now draw the apartment. You can draw two or three versions to show how the walls convert the space. Label the spaces with the function.

C Show your design to your partner. Explain the function of each space. Does your partner like the design? Does he or she have ideas for improvements?

Challenge! What does Larson think we need to change about transportation in cities? Watch his full talk at TED.com and choose the best answer.

- Save space
- Improve transportation
- Share resources
- Use advanced technology

Possessions

A woman in Italy inspects a plastic fish head that she received as a gift from her town.

UNIT 4 GOALS

1. Identify personal possessions

2. Talk about other people's possessions

3. Buy a present

4. Talk about special possessions

Vocabulary

A Complete the names of the objects in the pictures. Use the words in the box.

> book   pen   watch   bag   glasses   backpack
> wallet   ring   keys   necklace   dictionary   notebook

▲ **1.** b o o k

▲ **2.** n o t b o o k

▲ **3.** d i c t i o n a r y

▲ **4.** b a g

▲ **5.** p e n

▲ **6.** w a t c h

▲ **7.** b a c k p a c k

▲ **8.** w a l l e t

▲ **9.** r i n g

▲ **10.** n e c k l a c e

▲ **11.** g l a s s e s

▲ **12.** k e y s

B 🔄 Take turns. Find the differences between the two pictures.

> There are glasses in my picture.

> There are no glasses in my picture, but there's a cell phone.

Student A

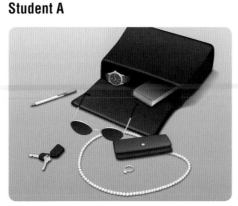

Student B

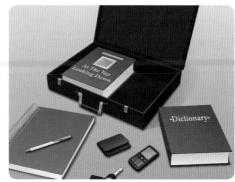

Grammar: Demonstrative adjectives

	Singular	Plural
Near ☞	**This** is your bag.	Are **these** your books?
Far ☞	**That** is not your bag.	**Those** are not my pens.

1.

A Match the questions and the answers. There can be more than one correct answer.

Question

1. Is this your pen? ___c___
2. Are those your keys? ___a___
3. Are these your glasses? ___d___
4. Is that your dictionary? ___b___

Answer

a. Yes, they are.
b. No, it isn't.
c. Yes, it is.
d. No, they aren't.

2.

B Look at the pictures. Use the cues to write questions.

1. (far) Are those your glasses?
2. (far) Are that your book?
3. (near) Are this your house?
4. (near) Are these your dogs?
5. (far) Are those your bags.

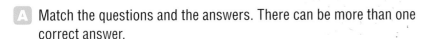

3.

Conversation

A  20 Listen to the conversation. What is in the bag?

Andrea:	Where's my bag?
Jennifer:	Is *this* it?
Andrea:	No, my bag is black.
Jennifer:	Well, is *that* it? It's black.
Andrea:	Is there <u>a bracelet</u> in it?
Jennifer:	Let me see. There's <u>a book, a dictionary, a pen, . . . a bracelet</u>!
Andrea:	Great! That's my bag. Thanks!

4.

B Practice the conversation with a partner. Switch roles and practice it again.

C Change the underlined words and make a new conversation.

D **GOAL CHECK** ✔ **Identify personal possessions**

Tell a partner what is in your bag.

5.

Grammar: Possessive nouns

Singular nouns	Plural nouns
Jim's bag Ross's father the student's homework (one student)	the students' homework (more than one student)

Listening

A 🔊 **21** Listen to Jill, then Lee. Circle **T** for *true* and **F** for *false*.

1. There is a cell phone in Jill's bag.   T   F
2. There is a dictionary in Jill's bag.   T   F

3. There is a cell phone in Lee's bag.   T   F
4. There is a notebook in Lee's bag.   T   F

B 🔊 **21** Listen again. Answer the questions.

1. What does Jill have in her bag that Lee doesn't have in his bag?

_____

2. What does Jill have in her bag that Lee has in his bag?

_____

3. What does Lee have in his bag that Jill doesn't have in her bag?

_____

C 🔄 Work with a partner. Take turns. Ask and answer the questions.

1. What does Jill have in her bag that you don't have in your bag?
2. What does Jill have in her bag that you have in your bag?
3. What does Lee have in his bag that you don't have in your bag?
4. What does Lee have in his bag that you have in your bag?

Pronunciation: /i/ and /ɪ/ sounds

A 🔊 **22** Listen and check the boxes. Listen again and repeat the words.

	/i/ sound	/ɪ/ sound
this		
these		
heat		
hit		
his		
he's		
sheep		
ship		

ship

sheep

Sounds in English can be written in different ways.			
/ɪ/ sound		/i/ sound	
Written	Example	Written	Example
i	kitchen	e	be
e	pretty	ee	sheep
ui	guitar	ea	teacher
		eo	people

B 🔊 **23** Listen and circle the word that you hear.

1. ship | sheep
2. it | eat
3. this | these
4. sit | seat
5. live | leave

Communication

A 🔅 Complete the following steps.

1. Write the name of an object on a small piece of paper. Give the paper to your teacher.

2. Your teacher mixes the papers and gives you someone else's paper.

3. Ask questions to find the owner.

B 🔄 **GOAL CHECK** ✓ Talk about other people's possessions

Ask a partner about what is in his or her bag. Share the information with the class.

> Excuse me, is this your watch?

> No, it isn't. I think it's Ling's.

> Yes, it is. Thanks a lot!

> Is there a pencil in your bag?

Language Expansion: Electronic products

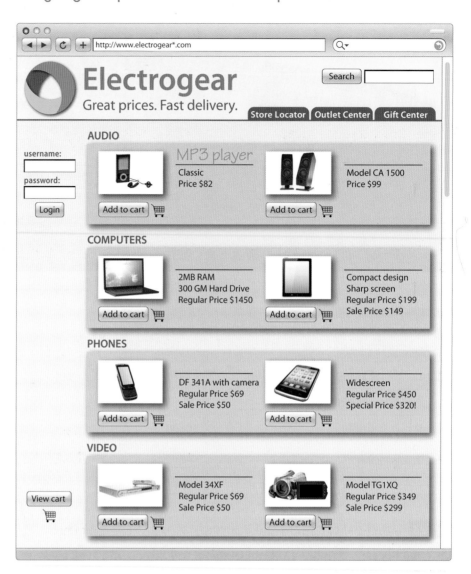

A Label the items on the Web page. Use the words in the box.

> camcorder   cell phone   tablet   speakers
> laptop   DVD player   smartphone   ~~MP3 player~~

B Read the Web page. Complete the sentences.

1. The camcorder is in the ___video___ section.

2. The _____ and the _____ are in the phones section.

3. The tablet is in the _____ section.

4. The MP3 player is in the _____ section.

C Write a wish list of the things you would like to have. You have $2,000 to spend.

Grammar: *Have*

Statements	Negative
I/You/We/They **have** a laptop.	I/You/We/They **don't have** a CD player.
He/She **has** a camcorder.	He/She **doesn't have** a DVD player.
Yes/No questions	Short answers
Do I/you/we/they **have** an MP3 player?	Yes, I/you/we/they **do.** No, I/you/we/they **don't.**
Does he/she **have** a cell phone?	Yes, he/she **does.** No, he/she **doesn't.**

A Complete the sentences with *have* or *has*.

1. Jim ___has___ a new laptop.
2. Do you ___have___ a laptop?
3. I don't ___have___ a cell phone.
4. Does Chen ___have___ a tablet?
5. Sofia ___has___ a smartphone.

B Write questions with *have* and complete the answer.

1. you | cell phone? ___Do you have a cell phone?___ Yes, ___I do.___
2. Alison | big house? ___Does He have big house.___ Yes, ___he does.___
3. you | my keys? ___Do you have keys?___ No, ___I don't___
4. Aki | a laptop? ___Does Aki have a Laptop___ Yes, ___she does.___
5. Mario and Dan | an apartment? ___Do we have an apartment___ No, ___they don't___

Conversation

A 🔊 24 Sun-Hee and Hana are buying a present for Sun-Hee's brother. Listen to the conversation. What do they buy?

Sun-Hee: Look at these new products!
Hana: Wow, these <u>cameras</u> look cool. And cheap!
Sun-Hee: My brother already has a good <u>camera</u>.
Hana: Does he have <u>a smartphone</u>?
Sun-Hee: No, he doesn't. Let's get <u>a smartphone</u>!

B 🔁 Practice the conversation with a partner. Switch roles and practice it again.

C 🔁 Change the underlined words and make a new conversation.

D 🔁 **GOAL CHECK** ✔ **Buy a present**

Work with a partner. Practice buying a present for a friend. Use the conversation and the Web site on page 48 for ideas.

▲ Most smartphones have cameras.

Real Language

We use *Wow!* and *Cool!* to show interest and excitement. Both are informal.

Reading

A  Write a list of your jewelry or the jewelry of a family member. Compare your list with your partner's list.

B Read the article. Then read the sentences. Circle **T** for *true* and **F** for *false*.

1. People wear jewelry for many reasons.   **T**   **F**

2. Aisha has gold earrings.   **T**   **F**

3. Aisha's father is a rich man.   **T**   **F**

4. Zhang Wei is giving his wife a ring.   **T**   **F**

5. Wang Changchang is happy.   **T**   **F**

C Answer the questions.

1. Does Aisha's family have a lot of money?

   _____.

2. How do you know?

   _____.

3. Are Zhang Wei and Wang Changchang married?

   _____.

4. Why is Zhang Wei giving a ring to his wife?

   _____.

5. Is Wang Changchang's ring made of gold?

   _____.

JEWELRY

In every country, people have jewelry. But why is jewelry important to people? Well, it is beautiful, but there are other reasons. Two of the most popular reasons are to say, "I am rich," or to say, "I love you."

This is Aisha, and she comes from Djibouti. She is from an important family, and her father has a lot of money—he is wealthy. Aisha has a lot of jewelry, and it is made of gold. She has gold earrings,

gold necklaces, and also gold jewelry that goes over her face. We can see she comes from a rich family because she has a lot of jewelry.

Zhang Wei and his wife Wang Changchang are from Beijing, in China. Zhang Wei is giving his wife a beautiful silver ring. They are in love, and they are very happy. The ring is a sign of Zhang Wei's love for Wang Changchang.

Communication

A 🔁 Answer the questions, adding one of your own. Fill in the first column and survey a classmate.

> **Do you have a tablet?**

> **Yes, I do.**

> **No, I don't.**

Do you have . . .	Me	Name: _____
a tablet?		
a laptop computer?		
a smartphone?		
a necklace?		
_____?		
What is your favorite possession?		

Writing Strategy

We use commas with **and** to make a list.

*Ampit has a tablet, a laptop, a desktop, **and** a smartphone.*

When we make a list, after a negative verb, we can use **or.**

*I don't have a tablet, a smartphone, **or** a laptop.*

To show contrast, we can use **but.**

*I have a smartphone, **but** Isabelle doesn't.*

Writing

A Write about what you and your classmate have and don't have. Use the information in the chart above with **and, or,** and **but.**

B 🔁 **GOAL CHECK** ✔ **Talk about special possessions**

Work with a partner. Tell your partner about a special possession. What is it? Where is it from? Is it old or new?

cave painting

Before You Watch

A 🔄 Work with a partner. Look at the pictures. Decide which of these things are interesting to archaeologists.

While You Watch

A ▶️ Watch the video. Check the things that you saw.

B ▶️ Watch the video again and complete the sentences using the words in the box.

> paintings   interesting
> skulls   old   slow

1. They are looking for ___old___ things.

2. Archaeologists study human remains, like these ___skulls___.

3. It is ___slow___ work.

4. Archaeologists also study ___paintings___ in caves.

5. Sometimes the work is dangerous, but it is always ___interesting___.

After You Watch

A Match the tools to the job. There can be more than one correct answer.

Tools

a. broom   **b.** ruler   **c.** brush   **d.** hammer

1. architect ___r___   2. artist ___brush___   3. archaeologist ___hammer and broom___

B 🔄 Compare your answers with a partner's answers. Discuss any differences.

▲ jewelry

▲ mummy

▲ pot

▲ plate

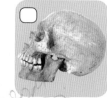

▲ skull

Daily Activities

People move quickly along the platforms at the Churchgate Railway Station in Mumbai, India.

Look at the photo, answer the questions:

1 Where do you go every day? **2** What do you do every day?

3

UNIT 5 GOALS

1. Tell time

2. Talk about people's daily activities

3. Talk about what you do at work or school

4. Describe a dream job

Vocabulary

Time	
5:45	five forty-five, a quarter to six
6:00	six o'clock
6:15	six fifteen, a quarter after six
6:30	six thirty, half past six

▲ get up

▲ take a shower

▲ start work

▲ finish work

▲ take a nap

▲ go to bed

▲ have lunch

▲ have dinner

A What time is it? Write the time.

1. It's five o'clock.
2. It's *twelve thirty, half past six*
3. *four fifteen, a quarter after four*
4. *two forty five, a quarter to two*
5. *ten thirty, half past ten*

B Complete the sentences with your own information.

1. I get up at _seven o'clock_.
2. I take a shower at _eight 30_.
3. I start work at _7:30_.
4. I have lunch at _9:0_.
5. I finish work at _4:30 PM_.
6. I go to bed at _10:0 PM_.

Grammar: Simple present tense—statements, negatives, and *What time . . . ?* questions

Statement	Negative	*What time . . . ?*
I/You/We/They **get up** at seven o'clock.	I/You/We/They **don't go** to work on Saturdays.	**What time do** I/you/we/they **start** work?
He/She **gets up** at seven thirty.	He/She **doesn't go** to bed at nine thirty.	**What time does** he/she **start** work?
*The simple present tense is used for actions that we do every day.		

Time expressions with the simple present tense	
every day/morning/afternoon/evening	**on** Sundays
at three o'clock	**at** night
in the morning/the afternoon/the evening	**on** weekdays/**on** weekends

A Complete the sentences. Use the verbs in parentheses.

1. Matt _____gets up_____ (get up) at eight o'clock on Mondays.
2. I _____start up_____ (start) work at seven thirty in the evening.
3. We _____don't take_____ (not take) a nap in the afternoon.
4. Wendy and Kate _____don't have lunch_____ (not have lunch) on Thursdays.
5. Dae-Ho _____finishes_____ (finish) work at two o'clock every day.
6. Hussein _____takes_____ (take) a shower at night.

B Unscramble the sentences.

1. take a nap   I   in the afternoon.
2. does not   at eight o'clock.   Helen   start work
3. at one thirty.   have lunch   We
4. morning.   I   every   take a shower
5. work   finishes   at five o'clock.   Paul
6. at night.   starts work   My father

I take a nap in the afternoon.
Helen doesn't start work at 8.
We have lunch at one thirty.
I take a shower morning.
Paul work finishes work at 5 o'clock.
My father starts work at night

Conversation

A 🔊 25 Listen to the conversation. What time does Marco go to bed on weekdays?

Abel: What time do you get up?
Marco: I get up at seven thirty on weekdays.
Abel: And on the weekend?
Marco: I get up at about ten o'clock.
Abel: And what time do you go to bed?
Marco: On weekdays, at about eleven o'clock, but on the weekend . . . late!

B 🔄 Practice the conversation with a partner. Switch roles and practice it again.

C 🔄 Practice the conversation again. Use your own information.

D 🔄 **GOAL CHECK** ✓ **Tell time**

Work with a partner. Ask and answer time questions about a friend or relative.

> **What time does your mother get up?**
>
> **She gets up at six thirty.**

▲ Joel Sartore at work

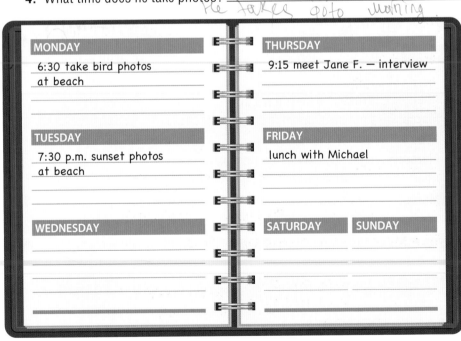

photographs by Joel Sartore

Listening

A 🔊 **26** Look at the pictures. What is Joel's job? Listen to the interview and check your answer.

B 🔊 **26** Listen again and answer the questions.

1. What is Joel's job? _____ photographs.

2. What time does he get up? He gets up 6:00. o'clock

3. What time does he take a nap? He gets 12:00.

4. What time does he take photos? to 11:00. He takes ooto maning

---

Word Focus

take a photo = use a camera

Word Focus

on Monday: on this particular Monday
on Mondays: on all Mondays

What do you do on Mondays?

I go to class at eight o'clock.

MONDAY		THURSDAY
6:30 take bird photos at beach		9:15 meet Jane F. — interview
TUESDAY		FRIDAY
7:30 p.m. sunset photos at beach		lunch with Michael
WEDNESDAY		SATURDAY SUNDAY

C 🔄 Take turns asking and answering questions about the planner above. Then ask and answer questions about what you do every day.

Pronunciation: Falling intonation on statements and information questions

A 🔊 27 Listen and repeat.

1. What time do you get up? I get up at six o'clock.

2. What time do they have lunch? They have lunch at one thirty.

3. What time does Bill go to bed? He goes to bed at eleven o'clock.

B 🔄 Take turns reading the following questions and answers to a partner. Use falling intonation.

1. What time does Salma start work? She starts work at eight thirty.

2. What time do they get up? They get up at a quarter to seven.

3. What time do you finish work? I finish work at six o'clock.

▲ In parts of Latin America, it is common for people to take an afternoon nap called a *siesta*.

Communication

A 🔳 Follow these three steps.

1. Write two more questions.

2. Answer all the questions.

3. Ask two classmates the questions.

What time do you . . .	Me	Classmate 1	Classmate 2
1. get up?			
2. have breakfast?			
3. start work?			
4. _____			
5. _____			

B 🔄 **GOAL CHECK** ✔ **Talk about people's daily activities**

Tell a partner about your classmates' activities.

> **Alison gets up at eight o'clock.**

> **She has breakfast at nine thirty.**

Language Expansion: Work and school activities

▲ check e-mail

▲ meet clients

▲ go to meetings

▲ travel

▲ talk to people on the phone

▲ go to the bank

▲ make photocopies

▲ write reports

A Write the work and school activities in the correct columns for you.

Things I do every day	Things I do every week	Things I don't do
I check my e-mail. I che..	J do	No, I don't..

B 🔁 What other things do you do at work or school? Make a list. Then tell a partner.

Grammar: Simple present tense—questions and answers

Question	Short answer
Do I/you/we/they **meet** clients every day?	Yes, I/you/we/they **do.** No, I/you/we/they **don't.**
Does he/she **meet** clients every day?	Yes, he/she **does.** No, he/she **doesn't.**

Adverbs of frequency

I **always** check my e-mail.	100%
I **sometimes** meet clients.	50%
I **never** answer the phone.	0%

A Match the questions and the answers.

Questions

1. Do you meet clients every day? _____
2. Does Ali make photocopies every day? _____
3. Do Chris and Helen travel a lot? _____
4. Does Hilary go to the bank every day? _____
5. Do you go to meetings every day? _____

Answers

a. Yes, they do.
b. No she doesn't. She goes every week.
c. No, I don't. I never meet clients.
d. Yes, I do. I always go to meetings.
e. Yes, he does.

▲ Singapore is a financial center in Southeast Asia.

B Write about your work or school. Complete the sentences using *always*, *sometimes*, or *never*.

1. I ___sometimes___ check my e-mail at nine o'clock.
2. I ___always___ go to meetings on Mondays.
3. I ___sometimes___ make photocopies.
4. I ___sometimes___ go to the bank.
5. I ___never___ write reports.

C Write three questions to ask your partner about what he or she does at work or school. Ask and answer questions with your partner.

Conversation

A ◀)) 28 Listen to the conversation. What does Brenda do at work?

Yoshi: Tell me about your work.
Brenda: Well, I'm a <u>personal assistant at a travel agency</u>.
Yoshi: What do you do at work?
Brenda: Oh, I <u>check my boss's e-mail. I make photocopies. I go to the bank</u>. It's not very interesting.
Yoshi: Do you travel?
Brenda: Sometimes. <u>I go to meetings with my boss, like to Rio and Singapore</u>.
Yoshi: Not interesting? It sounds fantastic to me!

B Practice the conversation with a partner. Switch roles and practice it again.

C Change the underlined words and make a new conversation.

D **GOAL CHECK** ✓ **Talk about what you do at work or school**

Talk to a partner about what you do at work or school.

Word Focus

boss = your superior, the person at the top

Real Language

We can use *like* to give examples.

GOAL 4: Describe a Dream Job

Reading

A What is the job? Match the job with the correct description.

> student   pilot   photographer   teacher
> explorer   filmmaker

1. I give students homework. _teacher_
2. I fly helicopters and planes. _pilot_
3. I make movies. _filmmaker_
4. I take pictures. _photographer_
5. I study and write reports. _student_
6. I travel to discover new things.
   explorer

B Describe a dream job to a partner. What daily activities make it more interesting than other jobs?

C Read the article. Circle the correct answer for each question.

1. What does Karen Bass do at work?

   (make films)   hunt wildlife

2. What does Karen film in the Altiplano?

   (the night sky)   bats

3. Why does Karen say she's lucky?

   People everywhere   She saves
   see her work.   animals.

4. Who does Karen have meetings with?

   (scientists)   (clients)

5. Karen takes a helicopter to film grizzly bears high in the mountains. Why do the bears live there?

   (to hibernate)   to look for food

> **WORD BANK**
> **behavior** habits or routines
> **environment** where you live
> **filmmaker** someone who makes movies
> **hibernate** winter sleep for animals
> **privileged** lucky

Ideas worth spreading

Karen Bass Filmmaker

UNSEEN FOOTAGE, UNTAMED NATURE

The following article is about Karen Bass. After Unit 6, you'll have the opportunity to watch some of Bass's TED Talk and learn more about her idea worth spreading.

Karen Bass is a **filmmaker.** She travels for work and makes films about wildlife. She tries to show animal **behavior** that most people never see.

Karen's job is not like most people's. When Karen wants to make a film, she starts by finding a new story to tell. Karen sometimes goes to meetings with scientists and experts, but she also travels to many places, such as the Altiplano in Bolivia, where she films the night sky. Karen's work for National Geographic's *Untamed Americas* shows a new species of bat in Ecuador. She works days, nights, weekends, and in hot and cold **environments.** The work is very hard, but Karen doesn't complain about it.

Karen also has a film about grizzly bears. The bears **hibernate** high in the mountains. Flying in a helicopter is the only way to get there. These amazing experiences make Karen like making films even more. Karen believes she's very lucky. She has a job that she loves and she gets to share something special with millions of people.

"I'm a very lucky person. I've been **privileged** to see so much of our beautiful Earth and the people and creatures that live on it."

– Karen Bass

Karen travels to beautiful places for her work, like the Altiplano.

Job Description: Travel Agent

Working Hours:
9:00 a.m. to 5:00 p.m,
Monday to Friday

Holidays:
Public holidays + 10
vacation days per year

Duties:
Answer the phone. Write
e-mails. Plan flights and
hotels. Send tickets to
clients.

A Read the job description. Travel agents help people travel to beautiful places like the ones Karen works in. Complete the paragraph below with the missing information.

This is a job description for a ___Travel agents___. The job is very interesting! You work from __9__ a.m. to __5__ p.m. and never on the weekends. The duties are to answer the phone, write e-mails, plan flights and hotels, and send tickets to ___clients___. The best thing about the job is the vacation days! You have ___Ten___ per year!

B Go back to the reading. Then complete the information about Karen Bass's job.

1. Job Description: _____
2. Working Hours: __every 9:00 a.m. to 5:00.__
3. Duties: _____ e _____

C Use the information from exercise **B**. Write a complete job description for Karen Bass in your notebook.

Communication

A 🔄 Share your description with a partner.

B 🔄 **GOAL CHECK** ✔ **Describe a dream job**

Tell your partner about a job you want to do. Use one from the list or choose your own.

– (wildlife) filmmaker   – helicopter pilot

– (wildlife) photographer   – scientist

Before You Watch

A Read the Video Summary. Use the words in blue to label the pictures.

Two dentists go to the San Francisco Zoo to treat animals. Their first patient is a sea lion named Artie. His teeth are fine. Then they examine an elephant named Sue. They check teeth in her mouth, and her tusks. Their last patient is a very difficult patient. Sandy is a black jaguar with a toothache. Her teeth are very bad and she needs surgery. The dentists have a very hard day.

While You Watch

A ▶ Watch the video, and then complete the sentences. Use *always*, *sometimes*, or *never*.

1. Dr. Sarah de Sanz _____sometimes_____ treats animal patients.

2. Dr. Brown's animal patients are _____always_____ dangerous.

3. Animals _____sometimes_____ have dental problems.

4. Artie _____never_____ brushes his teeth.

5. Humans and animals _____always_____ need good teeth.

After You Watch

A Which of these people might work in a zoo? Check (✓) the box.

1. ☐ a chef **4.** ☑ a doctor

2. ☐ an engineer **5.** ☐ a teacher

3. ☐ an artist **6.** ☑ a photographer

B 👥 Form a group and compare answers. Be ready to explain your answers.

1. _____

2. _____

3. _____

4. ___toothache___

5. _____

6. ___mouth___

Getting There

Traffic on Friday night in Seoul, South Korea, makes a colorful route.

UNIT 6 GOALS

1. Ask for and give directions

2. Create and use a tour route

3. Describe transportation

4. Record a journey

GOAL 1: Ask for and Give Directions

tourist office	train station
supermarket	post office
restaurant	hotel
museum	park
bus station	art gallery
library	movie theater

Vocabulary

A 🔄 Work with a partner. Locate the places on the map. Use the words in the box.

B Read the directions below and follow the red arrow.

> There is a tourist office on Grand Street.

Directions

You are in the tourist office. Go right and cross Lincoln Avenue. Walk two blocks to Long Avenue. Turn left and walk two blocks. Turn right and go into the museum.

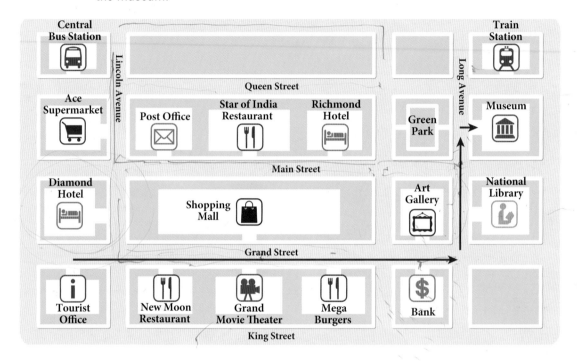

C Follow the directions and write the destination.

1. From the tourist office, turn right. At the corner of Lincoln Avenue and Grand Street, turn left. Walk one block up Lincoln Avenue. Turn right on Main Street, and walk one block. Cross the street. Turn right into _National Library_.

2. From Central Bus Station, turn left, then turn right on Lincoln Avenue. Walk one block to the corner of Lincoln Avenue and Main Street. Turn left on Main Street, and walk two blocks to the corner of Long Avenue and Main Street. Turn right, and on your left is the _Train Station_.

3. From the front of the Diamond Hotel, turn right on Lincoln Avenue, turn left on Grand Street, and walk two blocks to the art gallery. To your right is the _Bank_.

Real Language

To ask for directions, we say, *How do I get there?* or *How do I get to . . . ?*

Grammar: Prepositions of place; Imperatives

Prepositions of place	
on the corner of	The Diamond Hotel is **on the corner of** Lincoln Avenue and Grand Street.
across from	The art gallery is **across from** the library.
between	There is a restaurant **between** the post office and the Richmond Hotel.

A Use the map on page 68, and write the affirmative or negative imperative.

Affirmative	Negative
Turn right.	**Don't turn** left.

*The imperative is used for giving instructions.

1. To get to the shopping mall from the Grand Movie Theater, _cross_ (cross) Grand Street.

2. From the bus station, _turn_ (turn) left to get to the tourist office.

3. From the bank, turn left, and _walk_ (walk) one block to New Moon Restaurant.

B Use the map again, and write the correct prepositions.

1. The art gallery is _on the corner of_ Long Avenue and Grand Street.

2. The museum is _cross from_ Green Park.

3. Grand Movie Theater is _between_ Mega Burgers and New Moon Restaurant.

4. The post office is _across from_ Ace Supermarket.

▲ Big Ben is across the river from the London Eye.

Conversation

A 🔊 29 Listen to the conversation. Where does the guest want to go?

Hotel Guest: Is there a <u>supermarket</u> near here?
Receptionist: There's one <u>on the corner of Lincoln Avenue and Main Street, across from the post office</u>.
Hotel Guest: How do I get there?
Receptionist: OK. <u>Leave the hotel and turn right. Walk one block, and cross Lincoln Avenue</u>.
Hotel Guest: Thank you very much.
Receptionist: You're welcome.

B 🗪 Practice the conversation with a partner. Switch roles and practice it again.

C 🗪 Change the underlined words and make a new conversation.

D 🗪 **GOAL CHECK** ✔ **Ask for and give directions**

Work with a partner. Take turns asking for and giving directions using the map on page 68. Then take turns giving directions to places in your town or around your school.

▲ New York City,
United States

Listening

A Write the numbers of the stores on the map.

1. **Bergdorf Goodman** is on Fifth Avenue between East 57th Street and East 58th Street.

2. **FAO Schwarz** is on the corner of East 58th Street and Fifth Avenue.

3. **Barneys New York** is on the corner of East 61st Street and Madison Avenue.

4. **Tiffany & Co.** is on East 57th Street and Fifth Avenue.

5. **Bloomingdale's** is on Lexington Avenue between East 59th Street and East 60th Street.

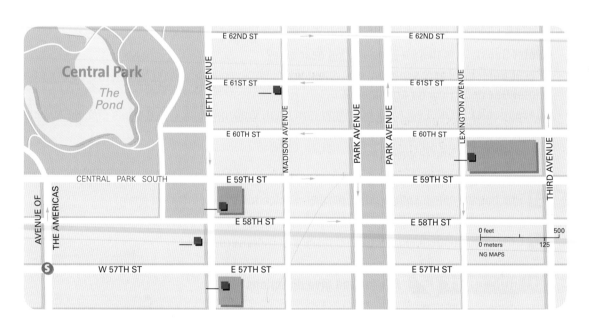

B 🔊 30 Listen. Draw the route on the map.

Pronunciation: *Yes/No* questions and short answers

A 🔊 31 Listen and repeat.

1. Is there a movie theater near here? ↗ ↘ Yes, there is. ↘

2. Is the bus station on York Street? ↗ ↘ No, it isn't. ↘

3. Is Barneys on the corner of East 61st Street and Madison Avenue? ↗ Yes, it is. ↘ ↘

B 🔁 With a partner, take turns reading the questions and answers.

A: Is there a hotel near here?

B: No, there isn't.

A: Is the library next to the museum?

B: Yes, it is.

A: Is there a tourist office in this town?

B: No, there isn't.

Communication

A 🔁 Use the map on page 70. Ask for and give these directions to a partner.

1. From Barneys New York to Tiffany & Co.

2. From Bergdorf Goodman to Barneys New York.

3. From Bergdorf Goodman to Bloomingdale's.

4. From Tiffany & Co. to Bloomingdale's.

B 🔁 In pairs, answer these questions about your town or city.

1. Is there a museum? What is it called? Where is it?

2. Is there a park? Where is it?

3. Are there good restaurants? Where are they?

4. What other places are interesting for tourists?

C 🔁 **GOAL CHECK** ✔ **Create and use a tour route**

With a partner, work together and write a tour route for your town.

▲ Rockefeller Center is between Fifth Avenue and the Avenue of the Americas.

Language Expansion: Ground transportation

From the Airport to Downtown

There are many ways to get downtown from the airport.

▲ **Bus**
Take the A100 bus to the Central Bus Station. $4.50

▲ **Taxi**
Take a taxi.
Approximately $50

▲ **Subway**
Take the subway direct to downtown. $2.50

▲ **Train**
Take the train. Change at Midway Station. $20

▲ **Car**
Rent a car. From $120 a day

▲ **Airport Shuttle Bus**
Take the airport shuttle bus to your hotel. $21–$25

A Complete the chart with the names of different types of ground transportation.

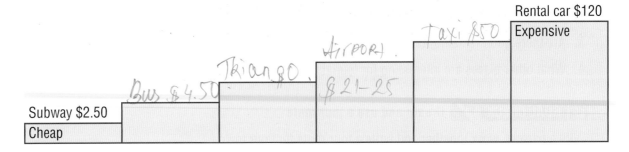

Rental car $120
Expensive

Taxi $50

Airport $21–25

Train $0

Bus $4.50

Subway $2.50
Cheap

How much is it to take the bus?

B Work with a partner. Ask and answers questions about how much it costs to travel from the airport using different types of transportation.

Grammar: *Have to*

Statement	Question	Short answer
I/You/We/They **have to** take a taxi.	**Do** I/you/we/they **have to** change trains?	Yes, I/you/we/they **do**. No, I/you/we/they **don't**.
He/She **has to** change buses.	**Does** he/she **have to** take a taxi?	Yes, he/she **does**. No, he/she **doesn't**.
*__Have to__ is used to show obligation.		

A Complete the sentences with the correct form of *have to* or *do*.

1. Do we ___have to___ take a bus? No, we ___don't___ take a train.
2. ___Do___ I have to change trains? Yes, you ___do___ .
3. ___Does___ Susan have to take the subway? No, she ___doesn't___ rent a car.
4. ___Does___ he have to go to the meeting? No, he ___doesn't___.
5. Do you ___have to___ get up at 9:00 on Sundays? No, I ___don't___ .

B Write sentences using *have to*.

1. Dan doesn't have any money. ___He has to go to the bank___ .
2. It's 3:00 and your train leaves at 3:30. ___I have to change train___
3. Mohamed goes to sleep at 10:00 and it's 9:30. ___He has go to bed___
4. I've got a toothache. ___I have to go hospital___
5. Ann's cell phone is five years old. ___She has to change cell phone___ .

▲ To get to Boston Logan Airport, you can take the subway . . . under the water!

Conversation

A ◀)) 32   Listen to the conversation. What time does the person have to get to the airport?

Tourist: Excuse me, how do I get to the airport?

Assistant: You can take <u>the subway</u>, but you have to change <u>trains</u>. It takes about an hour.

Tourist: Oh! But I have to get there by <u>two thirty</u>. And I have four bags!

Assistant: Two thirty! <u>In half an hour</u>? OK, you have to take <u>a taxi</u>! And quickly!

B 🔁 Practice the conversation with a partner. Switch roles and practice it again.

C 🔁 Change the underlined words and make a new conversation.

D 🔁 **GOAL CHECK** ✔ **Describe transportation**

Take turns giving directions from one place to another in your town. Say what transportation you have to take.

D GOAL 4: Record a Journey

Reading

A Read the diary and look at the pictures.

B Choose the correct answer.

1. The journey starts in ___b___.

   a. Elephant Island   **c.** South Georgia

   b. London

2. The *Endurance* breaks up on ___b___.

   a. October 26, 1914

   b. October 26, 1915

   c. October 26, 1916

3. ___b___ men leave Elephant Island on a small boat.

   a. Four   **c.** Six

   b. Five

4. It takes ___c___ to go from Elephant Island to South Georgia.

   a. one week   **c.** three weeks

   b. two weeks

5. Shackleton finds help in ___a___.

   a. Stromness   **c.** London

   b. Elephant Island

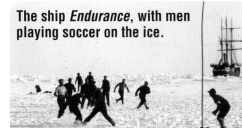

The ship *Endurance*, with men playing soccer on the ice.

Word Focus

break up = fall to pieces
help = assistance
rescue = save

JOURNEY TO
ANTARCTICA

1914

August 8 Ernest Shackleton and his men leave London on their ship *Endurance*.

1915

January 18 The *Endurance* is trapped in the ice. The men play soccer on the ice.

October 26 It's very cold. The *Endurance* **breaks up.** The men have to leave the *Endurance*. They camp on the ice.

1916

April 9 The ice starts to break up. The men have to get into the small boats.

April 15 They land on Elephant Island.

April 24 Shackleton and five men leave Elephant Island in a small boat to find **help.** The other men stay on Elephant Island.

May 8 Shackleton lands in South Georgia.

May 19 Shackleton leaves three men with the boat. He crosses the mountains of South Georgia with two men to find help.

May 20 They arrive in Stromness, the main town in South Georgia. They find help.

August 30 Shackleton **rescues** the men on Elephant Island.

London, England

Communication

A Read the European Tour plan below. With a partner, plan an itinerary to another part of the world. Think about the questions to the left.

Where do we want to go?

How long will we stay?

What do we want to visit there?

What will we do each day?

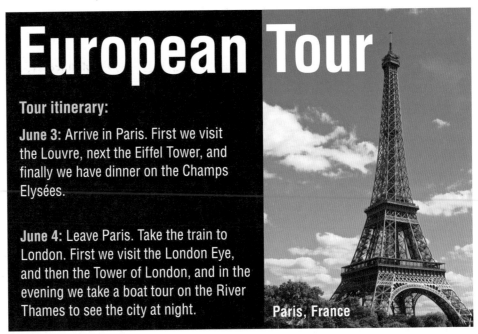

European Tour

Tour itinerary:

June 3: Arrive in Paris. First we visit the Louvre, next the Eiffel Tower, and finally we have dinner on the Champs Elysées.

June 4: Leave Paris. Take the train to London. First we visit the London Eye, and then the Tower of London, and in the evening we take a boat tour on the River Thames to see the city at night.

Paris, France

B Tell another pair about your plans.

Writing

A Now write your itinerary in your notebook.

B **GOAL CHECK** ✔ **Record a journey**

Think about your itinerary. In your notebook, write a diary entry about the trip. Share your diary entry with the class.

lava lake

crater

eruption

lava

magma

Before You Watch

A Study the picture. Use the labels in the picture to complete the text.

A volcano is a mountain with a large hole at the top. This hole is called
a _crater_. A volcano produces very hot, melted rock. When it is
underground, this hot, melted rock is called _magma_. When it leaves,
or comes out of the volcano, it is called _Lava_. When the lava stays
in the crater, it forms a _lava lake_. When lava leaves a volcano, we say
the volcano erupts. We call it an _eruption_.

While You Watch

A ▶ Watch the video. Match the sentence parts.

1. The geologists ___b___
2. The lava lake ___e___
3. Hot lava comes out of the earth ___b___
4. The team spends hours ___a___
5. It is not easy to stand near the crater ___d___
6. The professors are ___c___

a. collecting pieces of red-hot lava.
b. travel to the volcano on camels.
c. excited about studying the volcano.
d. because it is very hot.
e. is inside the crater.
f. and forms the lava lake.

▲ rocks and soil

After You Watch

A 🗣 Discuss these questions with a partner.

1. Do you want to explore a volcano? Why or why not?
2. How can people travel to difficult places?

TEDTALKS

Karen Bass Filmmaker
UNSEEN FOOTAGE, UNTAMED NATURE

Before You Watch

A Complete the sentences with the correct words.

camera

brush

books

tools

helicopter

1. This _____ is the filmmaker's.

2. Those _____ are the teacher's.

3. That _____ is the pilot's.

4. These _____ are the architect's.

5. This _____ is the artist's.

B Write the letter of the correct word to complete each sentence.

a. creatures	d. goose bumps
b. shoot	e. remote
c. den	

1. If a place is _____ it is far away from everything.

> Karen Bass's idea worth spreading is that new photographic technology is changing how we tell stories about animal behavior. Watch Bass's full TED Talk on TED.com.

2. A _____ is a place that animals use to sleep or hide.

3. You sometimes have _____ on your arms when you are afraid or excited about something.

4. To _____ something can mean to film it.

5. _____ are the same as animals.

C Look at the pictures and quotes on the next page. What do you think the TED Talk is about? What type of job is the TED Talk about? Discuss with your classmates.

While You Watch

A Watch the TED Talk. Read the quotes and look at the pictures. What do you see? Write the number of the picture on the line.

_____ **a.** Karen Bass uses a camera on a helicopter for her job.

_____ **b.** Baby grizzly bears walk with their mother.

_____ **c.** Karen Bass talks about her job.

_____ **d.** Baby bears roll down the mountain.

B Compare your answers from exercise **A** with a partner.

Challenge! Why do you think Karen's job is interesting? Can you think of other jobs where people travel a lot? Discuss with your group. Then share your ideas with the class.

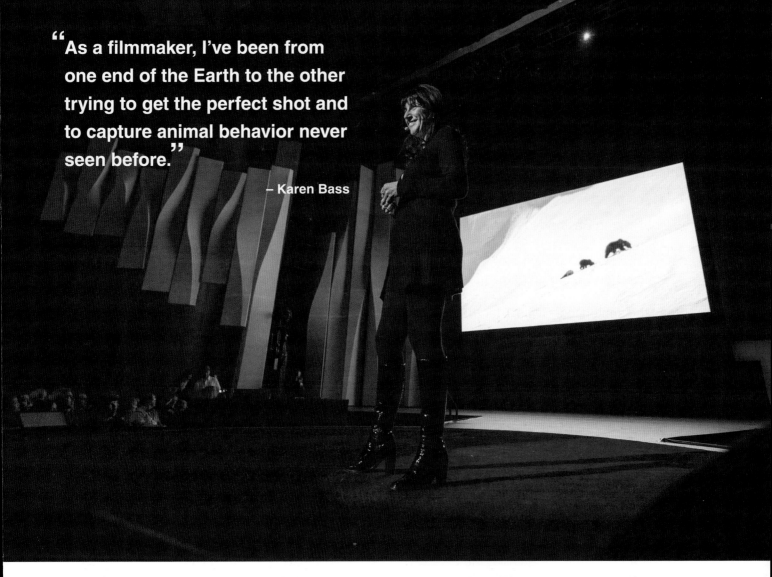

"As a filmmaker, I've been from one end of the Earth to the other trying to get the perfect shot and to capture animal behavior never seen before."

– Karen Bass

1. "Images of grizzly bears are pretty familiar. You see them all the time, you think. But there's a whole side to their lives that we hardly ever see."

2. "I love this shot. I always get goose bumps every time I see it."

3. "Getting down can be a challenge for small cubs."

4. "We film the video from a helicopter using a special camera."

TEDTALKS

Karen Bass Filmmaker
UNSEEN FOOTAGE, UNTAMED NATURE

A Watch the TED Talk. Match the questions with the answers.

Questions

1. Do the grizzly bears sleep in trees? ___

2. Does Karen Bass go to Alaska to make her film? ___

3. Do the grizzly bears climb mountains?___

4. Does Karen work at a travel agency? ___

Answers

a. Yes, they do.

b. No, she doesn't.

c. Yes, she does.

d. No, they don't.

B Read the sentences. Circle *T* for true or *F* for false.

1. Grizzly bears have dens.		T	F
2. Karen doesn't have a special camera.		T	F
3. Grizzly bears don't have cubs.		T	F
4. A helicopter has wings.		T	F
5. Mountains sometimes have a lot of snow.		T	F

C Work with a partner. What do you think? Discuss your answers to the questions.

1. Where do grizzly bears hibernate? Why?

2. Why do you think Karen films the bears?

D When Karen travels, she has to go to places she doesn't know. People in new places have to ask for directions. Locate the places on the map. Match the directions with the people.

1. The photographers have to go from the bus station to the museum. _C_

2. A hotel guest has to pick up her ticket from the travel agency. _d_

3. A college student has to meet his friends in the park. _e_

4. The banker has to buy his wife some jewelry. _b_

5. She has to meet her friend at the post office from the camera shop. _a_

a. Cross Grand Street. It's next to the Supermarket.

b. Cross Main Street. Go to the right. Turn left and walk down Grand Street. It's across from the Post Office.

c. Turn left on Long Avenue. Turn right on Main Street. It's across from the Italian Restaurant.

d. Turn right on Long Avenue. Turn right on Green Street. It's on the left.

e. Cross Grand Street. Turn right onto Lincoln Street. Turn left on Long Avenue. Turn right and walk one block down Green Street.

80

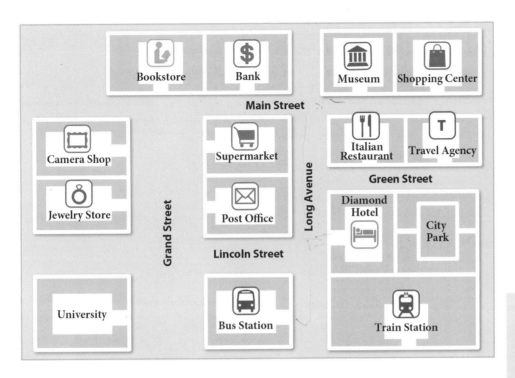

camera books
photocopy machine
car forest airport
streets school
office university
mountains plane

E Use the words to complete the chart. Write what each person *Uses* as part of their job and *Where* they work. Then, check if you *Like* or *Don't Like* the job. Some of the words can be used twice.

Job	Uses	Where	Like	Don't Like
Taxi Driver				
Professor				
Wildlife Filmmaker				
Personal Assistant				
Wildlife Photographer				
Pilot				

F Compare your chart with a partner's. Are your answers the same? Do you like the same jobs? Discuss.

Challenge! Find Alaska, British Columbia, and the Altiplano on a map or online. Are they close to each other? Make a list of the different kinds of transportation you think can be used to get to each place. Why do you think it is important to Karen to visit and show such different places in her work? Discuss with your group. Then share your ideas with the class.

Free Time

Divers explore a *cenote* in Mexico.
Cenotes are deep pits filled with water.

UNIT 7 GOALS

1. Identify activities that are happening now

2. Make a phone call

3. Talk about abilities

4. Talk about sports

Vocabulary

A 🔊 **2** Listen and write the words from the box under the correct picture.

> going to the movies   ~~watching TV~~   playing the guitar   reading
> shopping   going for a walk   listening to music   cooking

1. ___watching TV___

2. _____

3. _____#ʌ___

4. _____

5. _____

6. _____

7. _____

8. _____

B Write the activities from exercise **A** in a chart in your notebook. Your chart should look like this:

I like	I don't like
I Like I am reading	

Grammar: Present continuous tense

Statement (negative)	*Yes/No* question	Short answer	*Wh-* question
I **am (not) reading.**	**Am** I **reading?**	Yes, **I am.** No, **I'm not.**	Where **am** I **going?**
You/We/They **are (not) reading.**	**Are** you/we/they **reading?**	Yes, you/we/they **are.** No, you/we/they **aren't.**	What **are** you/we/they **doing?**
He/She **is (not) reading.**	**Is** he/she **reading?**	Yes, he/she **is.** No, he/she **isn't.**	What **is** he/she **doing?**

*We use the present continuous tense to talk about things that are happening at the moment.

A Unscramble the words to write sentences and questions.

1. the guitar.   is playing   Charlie   _Charlie is playing the guitar_
2. Marian   watching TV.   is not   _Marian is not waching TV_
3. Asha   listening to music?   Is   _Is Asha listening to music?_
4. Ju   What   reading?   is   _What is Ju reading?_

B 🗣 Work with a partner. Describe the picture at the top of the page. Take turns to ask and answer questions.

> **What is he/she doing?**

Conversation

A 🔊 3 Listen to the phone call. What is Dave doing?

Dave: Hi, Mom.
Mom: <u>Dave</u>! Where are you? What are you doing?
Dave: Mom, don't worry! I'm at <u>Paul's</u>. We're <u>listening to music</u>.
Mom: Well, don't be home late.
Dave: Mom, I'm <u>17</u> years old. Relax!

B 🗣 Practice the conversation with a partner. Switch roles and practice it again.

C 🗣 Change the underlined words and make a new conversation.

D 🗣 **GOAL CHECK** ✔ **Identify activities that are happening now**

Work with a partner. Look at the pictures on page 84. Ask and answer questions. Then look around the room and describe what people are doing and not doing.

Listening

A 🔊 4 Look at the pictures and listen to the telephone conversations. In what order do you hear the conversations? Write the numbers.

B 🔊 4 Answer the questions. Listen again to check your answers.

1. What is Mr. Evans doing? _He is talking another (Kelen) line_

2. Is David's wife taking a walk? _She is not meeting cla_

3. What is she doing? _She is meeting some clients_

4. Is Salma playing the guitar? _No. She isn't_

5. What is she doing? _She listening to music_

6. What is Tracey doing? _She is driving? talking_

7. Why doesn't Kenny want to talk? _driving   it's tak. dangerous_

Real Language

Useful telephone expressions.
Who is calling/speaking, please?
Can/Could I call you back?
Sorry, can/could you speak up?
Can/Could I leave a message?

C What telephone expressions can you use in the following situations?

1. You can't hear someone. _____

2. You don't know the caller. _____

3. You are busy and can't talk. _____

4. The person you are calling is not available. _____

Pronunciation: /ʃ/ and /tʃ/ sounds

A 🔊 **5** Listen and check the word you hear.

1. watch ✓   wash
2. cheap   sheep
3. chair   share
4. chip   ship

5. cash   catch
6. chop   shop
7. choose   shoes

B 🔄 Take turns reading the words. Your partner points to the words you say.

Communication

A Look at the chart. Fill in your information to make it true for you.

Day	Time	Location	Activity
Friday	8:00 a.m.	on the train	going to school
	1:00 p.m.		
	8:00 p.m.		
Saturday	8:00 a.m.		
	3:00 p.m.		
	8:00 p.m.		

B 🔄 Choose a day and time from the chart. Role-play a phone call with your partner. Follow the model below. Change partners and repeat.

Hi. Where are you? What are you doing?

I'm watching the soccer game! Can I call you back?

Wait, who is winning?

C 🔄 **GOAL CHECK** ✓ **Make a phone call**

Work with a partner. Take turns talking about what a friend or family member is doing right now.

| ice skate   ski   play soccer |
| play tennis   play volleyball |
| play golf   swim   ride a bike |

Language Expansion: Sports

A Match the words in the box to the pictures.

1. _swim_   2. _play soccer_   3. _ride bike_   4. _volleyball_

5. _ski_   6. _ice skate_   7. _play golf_   8. _play tennis_

B Answer the questions. Then interview two classmates.

Do you . . .	Me	Classmate 1	Classmate 2
play soccer?			
ski?			
ice skate?			
play golf?			
play tennis?			
swim?			
play volleyball?			
ride a bike?			

Spelling changes for verbs in the present continuous tense			
one-syllable verbs	**verbs ending in _e_**	**verbs ending with one vowel then a consonant**	
read – reading eat – eating	take – taking have – having	**one syllable** swim – swimming run – running	**two syllables** listen – listening finish – finishing

Grammar: *Can* for ability

Statement	Negative	*Yes/No* question	Short answer
I/You/She/We/They **can** swim.	He **cannot** swim. He **can't** play the guitar.	**Can** you ski?	Yes, I **can**. No, I **can't**.

A Write about yourself. Complete the sentences with *can* or *can't*.

1. I _____can_____ swim.
2. I _____can't_____ play soccer.
3. I _____can't_____ play golf.
4. I _____can't_____ ski.
5. I _____can_____ play tennis.

B Complete the conversations.

1. **A:** _Can you_ play volleyball?

   B: No, I can't, but I _can_ play soccer.

2. **A:** _Can yee_ Damien swim?

   B: Yes, _He can_ .

Pronunciation

🔊 6 Listen and check *can* or *can't*.

	can	can't
1.	✓	
2.	✓	
3.		✓
4.	✓	
5.	✗	✓

Conversation

A 🔊 7 Listen to the conversation. What can the new classmate do?

Julie: Hi, Yumi. I hear we have a new classmate.
Yumi: Yes, she's nice. She can <u>play the guitar</u>.
Julie: Wow!
Yumi: Yes, and she can <u>ski</u> and <u>ice skate</u>, but she can't <u>swim</u>. She's just learning.
Julie: Hey, I'm learning as well. Maybe I can invite her to my classes.
Yumi: Good idea. I'm sure she will like that.

B 🔁 Practice the conversation with a partner. Switch roles and practice it again.

C 🔁 Change the underlined words and make a new conversation.

D 👥 GOAL CHECK ✓ **Talk about abilities**

Ask questions to find someone in your class who can do TWO of the following: play the guitar, swim, cook dinner, ice skate, or play golf. Then tell the class about the person you found.

Can you ski?

No, I can't, but I can ice skate.

Free Time 89

Reading

A 🔄 With a partner, answer these questions.

1. Is soccer popular in your country?
2. Do you play soccer?
3. Do you have a favorite team?
4. Who is your favorite soccer star?

B Read the article and answer the questions.

1. Who is Pelé?
   He is soccer player

2. How many people in the world play soccer?
   264 million

3. Can women play soccer?
   Yes, can

4. What equipment do you need to play soccer?
   is a ball

5. Why is soccer so popular?
   anyone can play soccer

C 🔄 Can you guess what the top five sports in the world are? Work with a partner. Your teacher has the answers.

D 🔧 As a class discuss why you think these sports are popular.

E 🔄 Write a list of your top five favorite sports. Compare with your partner. Explain why you like these sports.

Word Focus

equipment = things used for an activity

famous = very well known

SOCCER— THE BEAUTIFUL GAME

In 1977, the **famous** soccer player Pelé named his book *My Life and the Beautiful Game*. The Beautiful Game is, of course, soccer.

Soccer is the number one sport in the world. According to FIFA, 264 million people play soccer. But that is just people who *play* soccer. About 3.2 billion people watched the 2010 World Cup on television. That is a lot of people. In fact, it is almost half the people in the world.

So, why is soccer the number one game in the world? Well, anyone can play soccer. Women, men, girls, and boys can play. Even Buddhist monks play!

Also, you can play soccer anywhere. You can play soccer on the beach, in your backyard, or in a stadium. And, unlike many other sports, you do not need special **equipment**—all you need is a ball. You don't even need special shoes. You can play in sandals, like the Buddhist monks.

▲ A woman skis down a mountain at the end of the day.

Writing

A Pick your favorite sport. Think of the rules. Write three things you can do and three things you can't do when you play the sport.

Sport: _____

Can:

_____

_____

_____

Can't:

_____

_____

_____

> You can kick the ball.

> Can you touch it with your hands?

Communication

A 🔄 With a partner, take turns asking and answering questions about your favorite sports.

B 🔄 **GOAL CHECK** ✔ **Talk about sports**

Work with a partner. Talk about your favorite sports. Say what sports you like to watch. Say what sports you like to play. Describe the rules to each other.

Before You Watch

A You are going to watch a video about a stunt bike rider. Circle five words you think you will hear in the video.

> slowly   walk   wall
> jump   fun   professional
> house   street

While You Watch

A ▶ People ride bikes for the following reasons:

exercise   fun   the challenge   money

Watch the video and circle the reason, or reasons, why Danny rides his bike.

B Answer the questions.

1. Where does Danny come from? _____
2. Where does Danny ride his bike? _____ 5 wall wall, anywere
3. Do people think Danny is good? _____ very good. professional.
4. What is Danny's challenge? _____

After You Watch

A Match the person and the challenge.

1. soccer player ___d___   **a.** get better grades
2. student ___a___   **b.** go faster
3. skier ___b___   **c.** hit the ball a long way
4. golfer ___c___   **d.** score more goals
5. basketball player ___e___   **e.** score more points

B 👥 Write down your own personal challenge. Form a group and ask others about their personal challenges.

A Sudanese woman wears a traditional *tobe*, which she wraps around her body.

UNIT 8 GOALS

1. Identify and shop for clothes

2. Buy clothes

3. Express likes and dislikes

4. Learn about clothes and colors

95

Vocabulary

> **This is a white shirt.**

▲ shirt

▲ dress

▲ jacket

▲ jeans

▲ shoes

▲ pants

▲ sweater

▲ tie

▲ hat

▲ skirt

A 🔁 Look at the picture. Then take turns describing the pictures below to a partner.

B Look at the pictures on the next page. Complete the sentences. Notice the words in **blue**.

1. Ruben is **trying on** black _____ shoes _____.
2. Lucy is **paying for** the _____ jacket _____ **by credit card**.
3. The sales assistant is **bringing** more _____ pink sweaters _____.

C 🔁 Work with a partner. Take turns describing what the people are wearing in the pictures.

Grammar: *Can/Could* (polite requests)

Wear is the verb you use with clothing.

Can/Could	
Can I try it on, please?	**Could** you bring another, please?
*Could is more formal than *can*.	

A Write the polite requests.

1. You are looking at two dresses, a red one and a blue one. You want to try on the blue dress. *Can I try on the blue dress, please?*

2. You want to see some red shoes. *Can I try on the red shoes, please?*

3. You want to pay by credit card. *Can I try on the this in a credit card, please? Can I pay by credit card?*

4. You are looking at two sweaters, a red one and a green one. You want to try on the green sweater. *Can I pay on the green sweater, please?*

5. You want the sales assistant to bring a size 7. *Can I try could you bring a size 7, please?*

Conversation

A 🔊 8 Listen to the conversation. What color sweater does the customer want?

Customer:	Do you have any <u>white sweaters</u>?
Sales Assistant:	Yes, we do.
Customer:	Could I see <u>them</u>, please?
Sales Assistant:	Yes, of course.
Customer:	Ah, <u>this one looks</u> nice. Can I try <u>it</u> on, please?
Sales Assistant:	Sure. The changing rooms are over here.
Customer:	OK. Back in a minute . . . . It fits great. I'll take it!

We can show we agree by saying:
Formal ←———→ Informal
Of course   Yes   Sure

B 🔁 Practice the conversation with a partner. Switch roles and practice it again.

C 🔁 Change the underlined words and make a new conversation.

D 🔁 **GOAL CHECK** ✓ **Identify and shop for clothes**

Work with a partner. Take turns role-playing a sales assistant and a customer trying on clothes.

Listening

A 🔊 9 Listen to the conversations. Number them in the order you hear them.

B 🔊 9 Listen again. In which conversation do you hear these expressions?

1. ☑ The sale price is $29.99.

2. ☑ Do you want to pay by cash or credit card?

3. ☑ How much are they?

4. ☑ What size are you?

5. ☑ That's $36 in all.

C Match the questions and the answers.

1. Do you want to pay by cash or credit card? ____b____

2. What size are you? ____a____

3. Can I help you? ____e____

4. How much is it? ____c____

5. Do you have this in black? ____d____

a. I'm a 12.

b. I'll pay by credit card.

c. The sale price is $35.

d. No, I'm sorry. Only in brown.

e. Yes, I'm looking for a red tie.

Pronunciation: *Could you*

A 🔊 **10** Listen and check (✓) the box of the form you hear.

	Full form	Reduced form
1. Could you call a taxi, please?	✓	
2. Could you call a taxi, please?		✓
3. Could you help me, please?		✓
4. Could you help me, please?	✓	
5. Could you repeat that, please?	✓	
6. Could you repeat that, please?		✓

The full form of *could you* is pronounced like "kud yu" (/kʊd ju/) and the reduced form is like "kudye" (/kʊdʒə/). The full form is used in formal speech and the reduced form is more informal.

B 🔁 With a partner, take turns reading the following sentences using the reduced form.

1. Could you bring me another pair of shoes, please?
2. Could you pass the water, please?
3. Could you say that again, please?
4. Could you tell me the time, please?
5. Could you bring my red scarf, please?
6. Could you repeat that, please?

Communication

A Complete the shopping list.

My shopping list			
clothes I would like to buy	shoes		
color	red		
size	8		
maximum price	$60		

B 🔁 **GOAL CHECK** ✓ **Buy clothes**

With a partner, role-play buying the clothes in exercise **A**. First, Student A is the customer and Student B is the sales assistant. Then switch roles.

1. _beige_ coat

2. _gray_ socks

3. _dark purple_ blouse

4. _dark pink_ scarf

5. _orange_ T-shirt

Language Expansion: More clothes and colors

gray brown light blue light purple

SAVONNETTE 100G 1€50

orange dark purple beige pink dark pink

A Write the colors of the clothes shown in the pictures.

B Write all the clothes you can think of in the correct column.

Clothes men wear	Clothes women wear	Clothes men and women wear	
coat shirt jeans jacket tie pants sweater hat	dress scarf skirt blouse socks	jeans scarf T-shirt shirt socks hat	jacket pants shoes

Grammar: Likes and dislikes

Likes and dislikes	
☺☺	I **love** jeans.
☺	I **like** pink T-shirts.
☹	I **don't like** hats.
☹☹	I **hate** white socks.
*We use these expressions to express likes and dislikes.	

A Complete the first column of the chart with other things like food, sports, and places. Then check (✓) the columns to show your likes and dislikes.

	☺☺ I love . . .	☺ I like . . .	☹ I don't like . . .	☹☹ I hate . . .
1. jeans	✓	✓		
2. the color red	✓	✓		
3. blue clothes			✗	
4. *gray sweater*	✓	✓	✓	
5. *black pants*		✓		
6. *orange shirt*		✓	✓	
7. *yellow clothes*		✓		
8. *scarf*	✓		✓	

B Ask your partner's opinions about your chart. Write an ✗ in the chart for your partner's answers.

> **Do you like strawberry ice cream?**

> **Yes, I love it!**

C Report to the class.

> **I hate strawberry ice cream, but Rafael loves it.**

Conversation

A 🔊 11 Chung and Brenda are buying a present for Brenda's brother. Listen to the conversation. What present do they buy?

Chung: What clothes does he like?
Brenda: He likes casual clothes. Jeans and T-shirts, you know.
Chung: What colors does he like?
Brenda: He loves dark colors. He hates colors like yellow or white.
Chung: OK, so buy him a black T-shirt.

▲ a present

B 🔄 Practice the conversation with a partner. Switch roles and practice it again.

C 🔄 Practice the conversation again, but buy a present for a person that you both know.

> **What things do you love?**

> **I love basketball.**

D 🔄 **GOAL CHECK** ✓ **Express likes and dislikes**

Tell a partner about things you love and things you hate.

Reading

A Tell a partner your favorite clothes color.

B Read the article. Match the word and the definition.

1. chameleon _b_   **a.** a person who fights in a war

2. invisible _d_   **b.** an animal that changes color

3. to change _e_   **c.** the part of the body you can see

4. soldier _a_   **d.** something you can't see

5. skin _c_   **e.** to make something different

C Circle **T** for *true* and **F** for *false*.

1. Chameleons change color when they are angry.   (T) F

2. Dark blue is a powerful color.   (T) F

3. Pink is the color of love.   (T) F

4. You can buy clothes that change color.   T (F)

5. Soldiers are invisible.   T (F)

D The reading says some colors make a person look a certain way. Do you agree? What do other colors say? Discuss with a partner.

Word Focus

calm = quiet

powerful = strong

romantic = loving

CHAMELEON CLOTHES

Chameleons can change the color of their skin. Sometimes they change color so that they are difficult to see and become almost invisible. Sometimes they change color to show that they are angry, or happy, or looking for a partner.

Of course, humans can't change the color of their skin, but we can change our clothes. Dark clothes make a person look more **powerful.** Pink is **romantic;** blue is **calm.** The color of your clothes says a lot about you.

Scientists are working on clothes that can change color when you press a button. They are not ready yet, but the idea is to make pants that can change from white to black or a shirt that can change from white to pink or red. Chameleon clothes!

Clothes that change color are also useful for soldiers. Like the chameleon, soldiers sometimes need to be invisible. Chameleon clothes make the soldiers difficult to see.

So, maybe someday you will be able to change your clothes from powerful to romantic to invisible—at the press of a button!

Communication

A  Take turns asking a partner about the clothes in the pictures. Use the questions to the left.

What is she wearing?

What color is it?

Do you like it?

Where do you think she is going?

Writing

A Write a description of the pictures.

She is wearing a yellow coat . . .

_____

_____

_____

_____

_____

_____

_____

_____

B GOAL CHECK ✓ **Learn about clothes and colors**

Ask your partner the following questions.

1. What is your favorite color?

2. What are your favorite clothes?

Then describe your style to your partner. What do you think your style says about you?

Before You Watch

A Match the opposites.

1. noisy _b_
2. same _a_
3. slowly _d_
4. modern _e_
5. beautiful _ugly_

a. different
b. quiet
c. ugly
d. quickly
e. ancient

While You Watch

A ▶ Watch the video and circle **T** for *true* and **F** for *false*.

1. Florence is a modern city.   T (F)
2. The factory manager is a man.   T (F)
3. There are lots of women working in the factory.   (T) (F)

▲ loom

B ▶ Watch the video again. Circle the correct answer.

1. The Industrial Revolution, (world wars, | the cold war, | world laws,) and floods forced change.

2. The mechanical looms were made (in 1780. | in the 19th century. | 500 years ago.)

3. Other manufacturers threw away their old hand looms (after World War I. | 500 years ago. | after World War II.)

4. The silk produced on antique hand looms has (4,000 threads. | 12,000 threads. | 3,000 threads.)

5. Every damask and brocade is (man-made. | handmade. | custom-made.)

After You Watch

A 🔄 Discuss these questions with a partner.

1. Why do you think Stefano Benelli is the only man in the video?

2. Are men better at some jobs than women? Are women better than men at some jobs? Why?

Eat Well

A baker in Iran is shown with all the food he eats in a day, some of it cooked in his bakery.

Look at the photo, answer the questions:

1 What food do you see in the picture?

2 What is your favorite food?

UNIT 9 GOALS

1. Order a meal

2. Plan a party

3. Describe your diet

4. Talk about a healthy diet

107

Vocabulary

▲ cereal and milk   ▲ eggs   ▲ steak   ▲ fish

▲ salad   ▲ pasta   ▲ chicken   ▲ fruit juice

▲ coffee   ▲ tea   ▲ chocolate cake   ▲ ice cream

A Write the foods pictured above in the correct place on the menu.

Breakfast
(7:00 a.m. to 12:00 p.m.)

Lunch & Dinner
(12:00 p.m. to 8:00 p.m.) All served with salad

Drinks

Desserts

B Tell a partner the foods you like and don't like for breakfast, lunch, and dinner. Use a dictionary if needed.

Grammar: *Some* and *any*

Some and any		
Statement	**Negative**	**Question**
There's **some** ice cream in the freezer.	We don't have **any** chicken.	Do you have **any** chocolate cake?

*We use *some* for questions with *can* and *could*. Can I have **some** water, please?*

A Complete the article with *some* or *any*.

In India, many people don't eat (1) _____ meat. They are called vegetarians. That means they don't eat (2) _____ chicken or (3) _____ steak. So what do vegetarians eat? They have (4) _____ delicious options. At an Indian vegetarian restaurant, you can order (5) _____ delicious fruit juices and enjoy (6) _____ wonderful salads. There are also (7) _____ great desserts.

▲ About one-third of the people of India are vegetarians.

B Unscramble the words to write sentences and questions.

1. some coffee   There's   on the table.   _____
2. some   I have   chocolate   Could   ice cream?   _____
3. have   We   don't   fruit juice.   any   _____
4. fish?   we have   any   Do   _____
5. eggs   next to   some   the milk.   There are   _____

Conversation

A 🔊 **12** Listen to the conversation. What does the customer order?

Waiter: Good evening.
Customer: Could I have some <u>coffee</u>, please?
Waiter: Sure.
Customer: Do you have any <u>strawberry ice cream</u>?
Waiter: No, I'm sorry. We don't have <u>strawberry</u>. We only have <u>chocolate</u>.
Customer: OK, I'll have some <u>chocolate ice cream</u>.

B 🔁 Practice the conversation with a partner. Switch roles and practice it again.

C 🔁 Change the underlined words and make a new conversation.

D 🔁 **GOAL CHECK** ✔ **Order a meal**

Change partners. Role-play ordering a meal.

▲ loaf

▲ bottle

▲ bag

▲ carton

▲ box

Listening

Miguel and Diana are planning a party. Miguel is writing a shopping list.

A 🔊 13 Listen and complete Miguel's shopping list.

_____ bottles of soda
1 bag of _____
20 _____
10 _____

B 🔄 Role-play buying the food on Miguel's shopping list.

loaf		bread
bottle		soda, fruit juice
bag	of	ice
carton		milk, eggs, fruit juice
box		cereal

> **Let's see. We need some soda.**

> **How many bottles do you want?**

C You are inviting some friends over for breakfast. Write a shopping list.

SHOPPING LIST
2 cartons of milk _____
_____ _____
_____ _____
_____ _____

Pronunciation: *And*

A 🔊 14 Listen and check (✓) the correct column of the form you hear.

	Full form	Reduced form
1. pasta and salad	✓	
2. pasta and salad		✓
3. fruit juice and cereal		
4. fruit juice and cereal		
5. chocolate cake and ice cream		
6. chocolate cake and ice cream		

B 🔁 With a partner, take turns reading the following sentences using the reduced form.

1. I like hot dogs and hamburgers.
2. Jill and David are good friends.
3. How many brothers and sisters do you have?
4. We have strawberry ice cream and chocolate ice cream.

Communication

A 👥 In groups of three, plan a dinner party.

1. Decide how many people to invite. Write down their names.
2. Make a menu for the dinner.
3. Decide where the guests will sit. Make a seating plan in your notebook.

B 👥 **GOAL CHECK** ✔ **Plan a party**

Join another group. Explain your menu and seating plan.

> **Word Focus**
>
> In conversation, the word *and* is often reduced to sound like *n*.

> Does Sachin eat meat?

> No, he's a vegetarian.

> Emmanuel can sit next to Leo. They are good friends.

> Let's put your brother between Gloria and Diana.

Language Expansion: Count and non-count nouns

The Eatwell Plate

The eatwell plate helps you to eat a healthy diet. It shows the types of food to eat and also how much of each type of food to eat. Do you see any of your favorite foods?

Count nouns . . .

. . . have a singular and a plural. *One apple, two apples.*

. . . take singular and plural verbs *The apple is red. The apples are red.*

Non-count nouns . . .

. . . only have a singular. *Water.*

. . . only take singular verbs. *The water is hot.*

A Write the foods from above in the correct column.

Count nouns (plural ending -s)	Non-count nouns
oranges	*rice*

B Add the names of other foods that you eat in your country to the chart in **A.**

Grammar: *How much / How many*

How much and *How many*	
Count nouns	**Non-count nouns**
How many oranges do you need?	**How much** milk do we have?
*How much and *how many* are used to ask about quantities.	

A Complete the sentences. Use *how much* or *how many*.

1. _____ eggs do you eat every week?

2. _____ meat do you eat every week?

3. _____ fruit juice do you drink every day?

4. _____ cookies do you eat every day?

5. _____ bread do you eat every day?

B 🔁 With a partner, take turns asking and answering the questions in exercise **A**.

Conversation

A 🔊 15 Listen to the conversation. Does the patient eat well?

Doctor: Tell me about the food you eat. How much fruit do you eat?

Patient: I eat <u>an apple</u> every day. Sometimes I have <u>an orange</u>, as well.

Doctor: Very good! Do you eat meat?

Patient: <u>Yes, I love meat.</u>

Doctor: How much meat do you eat?

Patient: <u>I eat a big steak every day.</u>

Doctor: And vegetables. Do you eat any vegetables?

Patient: <u>No, I don't like vegetables.</u>

▲ How many count and non-count nouns can you see at this floating market in Indonesia?

B 🔁 Practice the conversation with a partner. Switch roles and practice it again.

C 🔁 Change the underlined words and make a new conversation. Make the diet more healthy.

D 👥 GOAL CHECK ✔ **Describe your diet**

Make a list of the foods you eat on a normal day. Tell a partner or a group about your diet and decide with the group if it is healthy or not.

Reading

A Look at the pictures. Which foods are healthy? Which foods are unhealthy?

B 👥 Work with a group. Talk about the foods in exercise **A**. How many of these foods can you buy in your neighborhood? Where can you buy them?

C Read the article. Choose the words that correctly complete each sentence.

1. Ron Finley is an activist who likes to work in (gardens | restaurants).

2. He lives in a part of Los Angeles where there is a food (farmers market | desert).

3. In a (food desert | city), it is not easy to get fresh, healthy food.

4. In the (world | United States), more than 26 million people live in food deserts.

5. Ron Finley thinks that people should (eat more meat | grow their own food).

6. In South Central Los Angeles, there are many (vacant lots | empty streets) that can be made into gardens.

WORD BANK

access a way to get something
activist someone who works to solve a social problem
affordable does not cost too much money
garden area of land used for growing plants
gardener someone who takes care of a garden
vacant lot empty land in a city

Ron Finley Activist/Gardener

A GUERILLA GARDENER IN SOUTH CENTRAL L.A.

The following article is about Ron Finley. After Unit 9, you'll have the opportunity to watch some of Finley's TED Talk and learn more about his idea worth spreading.

Ron Finley is a **gardener** and **activist.** He lives in South Central, a low-income part of Los Angeles that Finley calls a "food desert." Food deserts are places with no access to fresh, healthy food.

How many people live in food deserts? In the United States, more than 26 million. In a food desert, people do not have **access** to food that is fresh, healthy, and **affordable.** There aren't many grocery stores or farmers markets. Instead, there are fast food restaurants and convenience stores. Many people in food deserts have bad health problems because of the unhealthy food.

Ron Finley wants to solve the problem of food deserts. He believes that people can grow their own food, even in the city. In Finley's neighborhood in Los Angeles, there are many **vacant lots** and other small areas of land that can be made into gardens. If there are **gardens** with vegetables and fruits, people will have access to healthy food and they can be more healthy.

Urban gardening helps people in the city get healthy food.

"Food is the problem and food is the solution."

– Ron Finley

D GOAL 4: Talk About a Healthy Diet

Finley says, "Growing your own food is like printing your own money."

WORD BANK

a. healthy
b. farmers market
c. dinner
d. ice cream
e. convenience store
f. favorite
g. potato

Writing

A Mia and her doctor are talking about what Mia eats. First, read all the sentences. Then complete the sentences with words from the word bank. Write the correct letter.

Mia says:

"I buy my (1) ___ foods at a (2) ___ near my house. For (3) ___, I eat pizza. Also I eat some (4) ___ chips. Later I eat a lot of (5) ___ ."

Mia's doctor says:

"Mia needs to eat more fresh, (6) ___ foods. She can buy them at a (7) ___ ."

Writing Strategy

When you write, it is important to self-correct. As you correct your own writing, you can use visual cues to help you focus on certain words. Some visual cues you can use are <u>underlining</u> and (circling).

B Do the sentences describe healthy or unhealthy eating habits? Discuss as a class.

C Mia wants to eat food that is healthier.

- Write a new paragraph about Mia, changing the unhealthy foods for healthy foods. *Mia buys… For dinner, she…*
- Underline the verbs and circle the subjects in your paragraph.

Communication

A Think of a place in or near your school where you could make a garden. With a partner, decide what you will plant there. Draw the shape of the area and mark it with the different plants. Decide how much or how many of each item you will grow.

- How many tomato plants do we need?
- Five tomato plants.

B GOAL CHECK ✔ **Talk about a healthy diet**

With a partner, plan a lunch menu. Use foods from your school garden.

Before You Watch

A Write the food in the correct column. Add some more food items.

~~hamburger~~   ~~cheese~~   fish   mushrooms   pizza   hot dogs   french fries   fruit

Fast food	Slow food
hamburger	cheese
pizza	*fish.*
hot dogs.	*mushrooms*
fruit.	*french fries*

While You Watch

A ▶ Answer the questions.

1. Is Greve a big city? _*it's a small*_
2. What do the people of Chianti produce? _*wine*_
3. Does the mayor want to change Greve? _*No, he do*_
4. What is the goal of the Slow Food Movement? _*keep good*_
5. What do the farmers of Pistoia produce? _*a special cheese*_

After You Watch

A How can you slow down your life? Label the pictures with the phrases in the box.

spend time with friends and family   eat healthy food
get more exercise   take a nap in the afternoon

B 🔄 Discuss with a partner: In what other ways can you slow down your life?

TEDTALKS

Ron Finley Activist/Gardener
A GUERILLA GARDENER IN SOUTH CENTRAL L.A.

Before You Watch

A Write the words from the box in the correct category.

carrots tomatoes ice cream pasta oranges hamburgers lettuce candy pizza beans

Garden Plants	Other Foods

B Look at the words in the box. Complete the sentences with the correct words.

food desert a place with no fresh, healthy food
garden land used for growing food
gardener a person that works in a garden
grow increase in size
plant to put something in the ground to grow
vacant lot an unused area of a city
volunteer a person who works for free; to do work for free

1. He will _____ some food in his _____.

2. The city has a _____ that has no markets or grocery stores.

3. She wants to _____ some tomatoes on the land.

Ron Finley's idea worth spreading is that we need to get smarter about the food we eat; and we should start by growing our own. Watch Finley's full TED Talk at TED.com.

4. The _____ was full of trash.

5. She is a _____ at the garden two days a week.

6. The _____ picked many vegetables from his plants.

C You are going to watch a TED Talk about Ron Finley's gardens in the city of Los Angeles. What do you know about gardening? Write down four things you think you will see in the TED Talk. Compare your list with a partner's.

While You Watch

A Watch the TED Talk. Place a check mark next to the items that you see in the talk.

_____ supermarkets

_____ wheelchairs

_____ clothing stores

_____ Central Park

_____ seeds

_____ money

_____ Ron Finley's sons

_____ orange trees

_____ volunteers

_____ children

_____ soccer game

_____ farmers' market

B Look at the pictures on the next page. Explain to a partner what you think is happening in each picture.

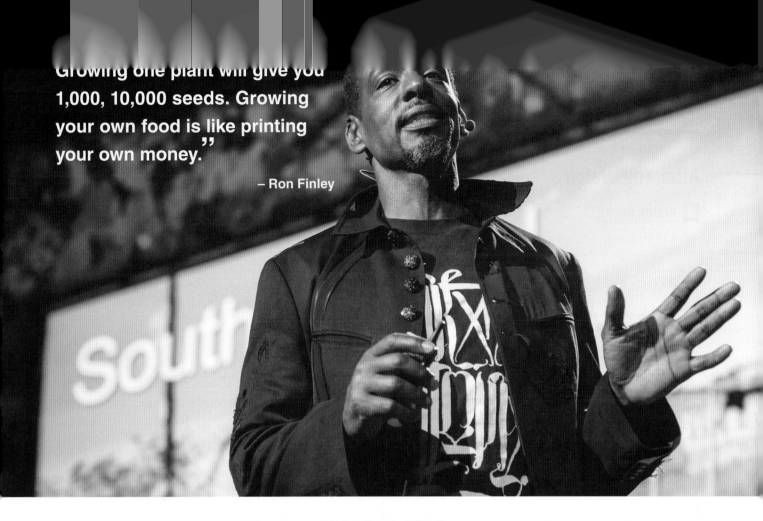

"Growing one plant will give you 1,000, 10,000 seeds. Growing your own food is like printing your own money."

— Ron Finley

"If kids grow kale, kids eat kale. If they grow tomatoes, they eat tomatoes."

"I have witnessed my garden become a tool for the education, a tool for the transformation of my neighborhood. To change the community, you have to change the composition of the soil. We are the soil."

USING VISUAL CUES

You do not need to understand every word you hear. Use visual cues such as photos in the TED Talk to help you understand the main idea.

"So with gardening, I see an opportunity where we can train these kids to take over their communities, to have a sustainable life."

119

TEDTALKS

Ron Finley Activist/Gardener
A GUERILLA GARDENER IN SOUTH CENTRAL L.A.

After You Watch

A Watch the TED Talk again. Choose the correct word to complete each quote.

1. More than 26.5 million Americans live in (Los Angeles | food deserts).

2. (Money | Food) is the problem and (food | water) is the solution.

3. L.A. leads the United States in (vacant lots | supermarkets) that the city actually owns. That's enough space to plant 725 million (tomato plants | apple trees).

4. One dollar's worth of (plants | green beans) will give you 75 dollars' worth of produce.

5. (Gardening | Shopping) is the most therapeutic and defiant act you can do, especially in the inner city. Plus you get (strawberries | vegetables).

6. If kids (want | grow) kale, kids eat kale. If they grow tomatoes, they (eat | buy) tomatoes.

B Are these statements true or false? Circle *T* for true and *F* for false. Correct any false information in your notebook.

1. Ron Finley saw that many people in his neighborhood were unhealthy.   T   F

2. Finley planted a food garden in the parkway in front of his house.   T   F

3. At night, hungry people took food from Finley's garden, so he stopped planting gardens.   T   F

4. Finley started L.A. Green Grounds, a group of volunteers who build farmers markets in the city.   T   F

5. Green Grounds planted about 10 gardens.   T   F

6. Finley believes that if kids learn to grow their own food, they will make the community better.   T   F

C 🔁 Work with a partner to explain how Ron Finley's gardens help solve each problem.

Problem	How gardening helps
1. Some people in South Central L.A. are unhealthy because of a poor diet.	
2. People do not have access to fresh, healthy food.	
3. The city has too many vacant lots.	
4. Kids do not have a sustainable way of living or healthy habits.	

D 🔁 Write a list of the healthy foods you eat. Compare your list with a partner.

E 👥 Work with a group to plan a small garden. Follow these steps:

- Say why your area should have a community garden.
- Use your lists from **D** to pick four foods that can be planted in the garden.
- Research the plants on the Internet or in the library to find out when they should be planted and what growing conditions (sunlight, weather, etc.) they need.
- Pick a place to build your garden. Plan your garden. Make a poster showing the garden's location and the foods that will be planted. Explain why you chose these plants.
- Present your garden poster to the class.

Challenge! Ron Finley is not the only person who believes that people need to grow their own food. Watch Roger Doiron's TED Talk on TED.com. How are their ideas similar? How are they different?

Health

Fan dancing is a beautiful form of exercise. These women perform a traditional fan dance in Shanghai.

Look at the photo, answer the questions:

1 Is exercise important to your health?

2 What do you do to stay healthy?

UNIT 10 GOALS

1. Identify parts of the body to say how you feel

2. Ask about and describe symptoms

3. Identify remedies and give advice

4. Describe how to prevent health problems

Vocabulary

A 🔊 **16** Listen and repeat the parts of the body.

B How are they feeling? Complete the sentences below with words from the box.

head
face   ear
chest   back
stomach   arm
hand
finger
knee
leg
foot/feet

▲ headache

▲ fever

▲ cough

▲ backache

▲ stomachache

| terrible   sick   OK   well   great |

tou.

1. John is ___sick___. He has a fever, a cough, and a bad headache.
2. Mary isn't ___great / well___. She has a stomachache.
3. Michael is ___well___. His fever is gone today.
4. Jane feels ___great___. She isn't sick, and today's her birthday.
5. Susan is feeling ___terrible___. She has a backache and can't move.

Grammar: *Feel, look*

Affirmative	Negative	*Yes/No* questions	Short answers	Information questions	Answers
I **feel** sick. He/She **looks** sick.	Hilary **doesn't feel** great. You **don't look** well.	**Do** you **feel** OK? **Does** he/she **look** tired?	Yes, **I do.** No, **she doesn't.**	How **do** you **feel**? How **are** you **feeling**?	I **feel** fine.
*The verbs *look* and *feel* are followed by an adjective. **The questions *How do you feel?* and *How are you feeling?* are interchangeable.					

A Match the questions and sentences with the responses.

1. How do you feel? _b_
2. Do you feel OK? _d_
3. Does Talib look well? _c_
4. How do they feel? _e_
5. Sarah doesn't look well. _a_

a. She isn't feeling well.
b. I feel fine.
c. No, he doesn't. He looks sick.
d. No, I feel terrible.
e. They feel OK.

B Complete the sentences.

1. **A:** Do you feel OK?
   B: Yes, I _do_ .
2. **A:** How is Melanie?
   B: She doesn't _look_ well.
3. **A:** How _do you feel_ ?
   B: I feel terrible.
4. **A:** What's the matter?
   B: I don't _feel_ well.
5. **A:** Does Gerardo look OK?
   B: No, he _doesn't look_ sick.

▲ Chicken pox affects many children. It causes blisters, fever, and headache.

Conversation

A 🔊 17 Listen to the conversation. What's wrong with Kim?

Boss: What's the matter, Kim? You don't look well.
Kim: I don't feel well. My head hurts.
Boss: Oh, no!
Kim: And I feel sick.
Boss: OK. You can go home.

B 🔄 Practice the conversation with a partner. Switch roles and practice it again.

C 🔄 You don't feel well at school. Ask the teacher (your partner) to let you go home. Then switch roles.

D 🔄 **GOAL CHECK** ✓ **Identify parts of the body to say how you feel**

Take turns asking a partner how he or she feels today. Be creative with your aches and pains.

Real Language

We can ask about someone's health by using these questions:

Formal ◄──────► Informal

What's the matter? *What's wrong?* *What's up?*

How are you? is a greeting. We do not normally use it to ask about someone's health.

Health 125

A doctor gives a baby a checkup.

Word Focus

We can say *I have a stomachache* or *My stomach hurts*.

We can use **hurt(s)** for other parts of the body (e.g., *my foot hurts, my fingers hurt*).

Listening

A 🔊 18 Listen to the conversations. List the patients' symptoms.

Patient 1	Patient 2
head, feet, knee, arm,	co. stomachache, fever

B Match the problems and the symptoms. Write the symptoms that go with each problem. You can use the symptoms more than once.

Symptoms

a. backache

b. fever

c. your arm hurts

d. headache

e. sore throat

f. cough

g. your knee hurts

h. toothache

Problems

1. cold: fever headache sore throat

2. flu: fever cough

3. bad tooth: toothache

4. car accident: backache headache arm knee hurts

Pronunciation: Sentence stress

A 🔊 **19** Listen and notice the underlined stressed syllables.

Doctor: How can I <u>help</u> you?
Patient: I don't feel very <u>well</u>. I have a <u>head</u>ache.
Doctor: Anything <u>else</u>?
Patient: Yes, I have a <u>fe</u>ver.
Doctor: OK. I think I need to ex<u>a</u>mine you.

B 🔊 **20** Listen to the conversation. Underline the
stressed syllables.

Dentist: How are you today?
Patient: I have a terrible toothache.
Dentist: Where does it hurt?
Patient: Right here.
Dentist: I see the problem.

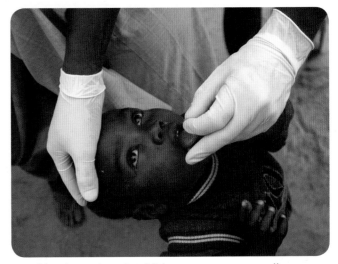

▲ Vaccines given to children can save many lives.

Communication

A 🔄 Role-play the following situations.

Situation 1	**Situation 2**
Student A	**Student B**
You are a doctor. Ask your patient how he or she feels.	You are a dentist. Ask your patient how he or she is.
Student B	**Student A**
You are the patient. You have a cough, a headache, and a fever.	You are the patient. You have a toothache.

Where does it hurt?

Does it hurt a lot?

Yes, when I eat or drink something hot!

B 🔄 Look at the pictures with a partner. Describe what is wrong with each child.

C 🔄 **GOAL CHECK** ✔ **Ask about and describe symptoms**

Look at the pictures above. Role-play a conversation between a doctor or dentist and these patients. Then switch roles.

Language Expansion: Remedies

▲ go to bed

▲ see a doctor

▲ lie down

▲ see a dentist

▲ take some cough medicine

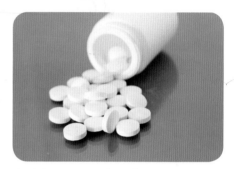

▲ take some pain reliever

A Answer the questions. Use the phrases above.

1. What do you do when you have a headache? *go to bed*
2. What do you do when you have a very bad backache? *lie down*
3. What do you do when you have a cough? *take some pain ret.*
4. What do you do when you have a toothache? *see a dentist*
5. What do you do when you have a fever? *take some cough*

Grammar: *Should* (for advice)

Statement	Negative	*Yes/No* question	Short answers	*Wh-* question
You **should** go to bed. He **should** take some cough medicine.	He **shouldn't** go to work today.	**Should** I see a doctor?	Yes, you **should**. No, you **shouldn't**.	What **should** I do?
*We use *should* to ask for and give advice.				

Some people get *seasick* on boats. People who are seasick get stomachaches.

A Match the questions and the answers.

1. I feel sick. Should I see a doctor? ___a___   a. You should take some pain reliever.

2. I have a headache. What should I do? ___d___   b. He should see a dentist.

3. Nelson has a toothache. What should he do? ___b___   c. She should take some cough medicine.

4. Should Uzra see a doctor? ___e___   d. Yes, you should.

5. Hilary has a cough. What should she do? ___c___   e. No, she shouldn't.

B Complete the conversations, and then practice them with a partner.

Pain Reliever
cough medicine

1. **A:** I have a backache. What should I do?   **B:** You should... *have some*

2. **A:** I think I have the flu. What should I do?   **B:** *You should take some cough md*

3. **A:** I have a stomachache. What should I do?   **B:** *you should see a doctor*

4. **A:** I have a cough. What should I do?   **B:** *You should take some cough medicine*

Conversation

A 🔊 21 Listen to the conversation. What does Casey think Brenda should do?

Casey: Hi. What's up, Brenda?
Brenda: I don't feel well. I <u>think I have the flu</u>. What should I do?
Casey: I think you should <u>go home and go to bed</u>.
Brenda: Do you think I should see a doctor?
Casey: <u>No, I don't think so</u>.

B 🔁 Practice the conversation with a partner. Switch roles and practice it again.

I have a toothache.

C 🔁 Change the underlined words and make a new conversation.

You should go to the dentist.

D 🔁 **GOAL CHECK** ✓ Identify remedies and give advice

Work with a partner. Take turns naming a medical problem and suggesting a remedy or giving advice.

Reading

A Check the things we can prevent. Compare your answer with a partner's answers. How can we prevent them?

- ☐ flu
- ☐ rain
- ☐ toothache
- ☐ headache

B Read the article. Circle **T** for *true* and **F** for *false*.

1. There is a vaccine for measles. **T** F
2. About 400,000 children die from malaria every day in Africa. T **F**
3. There is a vaccine for malaria. T **F**
4. Mosquito nets are expensive. **T** **F**
5. Influenza is a problem in hot countries. **T** F

C With a partner, talk about another disease you think we can prevent. How can we prevent it?

Word Focus

infectious disease = a disease you can get from another person

malaria = a sickness you can get from mosquitoes

prevent = avoid a problem before it happens

vaccine = medicine to prevent a disease

PREVENTING DISEASE

Many people, especially children, die from **infectious diseases** every year. We can **prevent** many infectious diseases. Let's look at some of the most dangerous ones.

Measles is mainly a children's disease. There is a very good, cheap **vaccine** for measles. All children should get the vaccine, but unfortunately not all do. About 900,000 children die every year from measles.

Imagine seven jumbo jets full of children. Now, imagine that all the jets crash and all the children are killed. That's how many children die from **malaria** in Africa *every day*. There is no vaccine for malaria, but it is not difficult to prevent. All you need is a $5 mosquito net.

Influenza (or flu) is caused by a virus. The virus changes, so scientists have to make a new vaccine every year. People at risk—for example, older people—should have a flu shot every year. In a bad year, influenza can kill millions of people.

Children and adults should sleep under a mosquito net.

All children should get
a measles shot.

Regular exercise helps prevent heart disease.

Writing

A Write a paragraph in your notebook about how to prevent one of the following health problems. Add your own ideas. Use a dictionary.

		wash fruit.
		eat candy.
To prevent toothaches, you		play sports.
		eat uncooked food, like salads.
To prevent heart disease, you	should shouldn't	go to the dentist every six months.
		exercise daily.
		eat healthy food.
To prevent stomach problems when you are traveling, you		brush your teeth after meals.
		eat lots of fast food.

To prevent toothache, you should brush your teeth after meals,

visit the dentist every six months, and you shouldn't eat candy.

Communication

A Choose one of the following. With a partner, discuss and write down three things you should do to:

prevent car accidents.

prevent accidents in the home.

get good grades.

B **GOAL CHECK** ✓ **Describe how to prevent health problems**

Present your ideas to the class.

Before You Watch

A Complete the Video Summary using the words in the box.

Video Summary

Farley is a red panda. He is cute, but he is a (1) _not live_. He nearly (2) _dies_ because his mother doesn't (3) _look after_ him. Then he gets very sick. Zookeepers give him _antibiotics_ and he gets better. Then they send him to another zoo to live with other red pandas.

> **antibiotics** = medicine that kills bacteria
>
> **die(s)** = not live
>
> **fighter** = someone who tries very hard
>
> **look after** = care for

While You Watch

A ▶ Circle **T** for *true* and **F** for *false*.

1. Farley grows slowly at first.   T   (F)
2. The zookeepers take Farley to the zoo's hospital.   (T)   F
3. Farley has the flu.   T   (F)
4. Farley likes his new friend, Banshee.   (T)   F

B In your notebook, correct the *false* statements.

> food   water   love
> education   success
> family   friends
> medicine   water
> sleep   a job   shelter

After You Watch

A Humans also have needs. Write the words in the box in the correct place in the chart.

B 🔄 Compare your answers with a partner and discuss any differences.

Self-esteem:	success,
Social:	a job, friends,
Safety:	shelter
Basic needs:	food, water, sleep,

Making Plans

A carnival ride lights up the night sky at a fair in Minnesota, USA.

Look at the photo, answer the questions:

1 What are your plans for the weekend?

2 What are your plans for your life?

UNIT 11 GOALS

1. Plan special days

2. Describe holiday traditions

3. Make life plans

4. Express wishes and plans

go to a game

▲ have a party

▲ have a barbecue

▲ go to the movies

▲ have a family meal

Vocabulary

	+
January	**May**
7th, Dad's birthday	14th, My birthday
February	**June**
17th, John's birthday	3rd, Mom's birthday
March	**July**
	24th, Grandpa and Grandma's anniversary
April	**August**
1st, Mom and Dad's anniversary	

A Look at the planner and the pictures. Decide the best way to celebrate. Complete the sentences.

1. Dad likes sports, so on his birthday, we usually _____
   _____ .

2. Mom and Dad like to eat outdoors, so for their anniversary, we usually
   _____ .

3. John loves films, so on his birthday, we usually _____
   _____ .

4. Mom doesn't like cooking, so on her birthday, we usually _____
   _____ .

5. I like to see my friends, so on my birthday, we _____
   _____ .

6. Grandma loves cooking, so on her and Grandpa's anniversary, we go to
   their house and _____ .

B 🔁 Tell a partner what you usually do on your birthday.

> What do you usually do on your birthday?

> On my birthday, I usually . . .

▲ go out to eat

Grammar: *Be going to*

Be going to			
Statement	**Negative**	**Yes/No question**	**Wh- question**
I **am going to** have a party.	We **are not going to** have a big meal.	**Are** you **going to** go to the movies?	What **is** he **going to** do? When **are** we **going to** go?

*We use *be going to* for making plans.
*We also use these time expressions: *tomorrow, next Saturday/week/year.*

A Complete the sentences. Use the words in parentheses and *be going to.* Then practice the conversations with a partner.

1. **A:** What _____ (you) do for your birthday?

   B: I _____ have a BIG party! People are going to give me presents.

2. **A:** _____ (you) have a barbecue on the weekend?

   B: No, we _____ go to the movies.

3. **A:** Where _____ (Courtney and Min) go on New Year's Eve?

   B: They _____ go to Santo Domingo.

B Discuss these questions with your partner.

1. What are you going to do after class?

2. What are you going to do this weekend?

Conversation

A 🔊 22 Listen to the conversation. When is Susan's birthday?

Sally: When is your birthday?
Susan: It's on <u>May 21st</u>.
Sally: Hey, that's next week. Are you going to <u>have a party</u>?
Susan: No, I'm going to <u>go out for dinner with my parents</u>.

▲ Santo Domingo is the capital of the Dominican Republic.

B Practice the conversation with a partner. Switch roles and practice it again.

C Change the underlined words and make a new conversation that is true for you.

D 🔆 **GOAL CHECK** ✔ **Plan special days**

With a group, choose a special day, for example New Year's Eve or a graduation. Tell how you are going to celebrate it.

▲ On New Year's Eve in New York City, people go to Times Square to celebrate.

▲ All over the United States, people celebrate Independence Day with fireworks.

Listening

A Look at the pictures. Read the captions about American holidays.

American Holidays

▲ On Thanksgiving Day, many people have a family meal.

B 🔊 23 Listen and write which holidays the people are talking about.

1. Linda and Kenichi are talking about _____.

2. Tom and Maria are talking about _____.

C 🔊 23 Listen again and answer the questions.

1. Why isn't Linda going to go to Times Square? _____

2. What is she going to do? _____

3. Where is Kenichi going to go? _____

4. What are Tom and Maria going to do? _____

5. What time is Tom leaving? _____

Pronunciation: *Be going to* (reduced form)

A 🔊 24 Listen and check the correct column of the form you hear.

	Full form	Reduced form
1. We're going to have a party.	✓	
2. We're going to have a party.		✓
3. I'm going to go to Paris.		
4. I'm going to go to Paris.		
5. They're not going to come.		
6. They're not going to come.		

B 🔄 Practice the dialogs with a partner. Use the reduced form of *be going to*.

A: What are you going to do on the weekend?
B: I'm going to go to the beach.
A: Are you going to go to Kim's party?
B: No, I'm going to stay home this weekend.

Communication

A 🔄 In your notebook, write a list of holidays in your country. With a partner, discuss what you are going to do on those days.

▲ Chinese New Year is celebrated all over the world. People give gifts, light lanterns, and watch parades.

B ♻ **GOAL CHECK** ✔ **Describe holiday traditions**

Join another pair of students and tell them about two holidays on your list.

Language Expansion: Professions

▲ law

▲ information technology

▲ medicine

▲ music

▲ acting

▲ education

A Match the person to the profession.

1. nurse _____
2. lawyer _____
3. musician _____
4. software engineer _____
5. actor _____
6. teacher _____

a. music
b. medicine
c. education
d. acting
e. law
f. information technology

Grammar: *Would like to* for wishes

Statement	*Yes/No* question	Short answer	*Wh-* question
I **would like to** be a nurse. Danny **would like to** study law.	**Would** you **like to** study engineering? **Would** you **like to** be a nurse?	Yes, I **would**. No, I **wouldn't**.	What **would** you **like to** be?

A Unscramble the words to write sentences and questions.

1. to be a would like I musician. _____

2. Eleanor like What would to be? _____

3. to be Would you a doctor? like _____

4. Deng medicine. would to study like _____

5. What like to be? would you _____

B Write the wishes or plans. Add one of your own.

Wish

1. _I would like to be an actor._

2. Danny would like to study medicine.

3. _____

4. We would like to leave at seven o'clock.

5. _____

6. _____

Plan

I am going to be an actor.

_____

I am going to be a software engineer.

_____

They are going to study music.

_____

Conversation

A 🔊 25 Listen to the conversation. What would Wendy like to be?

Father: So Wendy, you're <u>18</u> years old today. What are you going to do with your life?

Wendy: Well, I'd like to get married and have children.

Father: Whoa! Not so fast!

Wendy: Just kidding! I'd like to <u>study law and become a lawyer</u>.

Real Language

We can say *Just kidding* to show we are not serious.

B 🔁 Practice the conversation with a partner. Switch roles and practice it again.

C 🔁 Change the underlined words and make a new conversation.

D 🔁 **GOAL CHECK** ✓ **Make life plans**

Talk to a partner. What would you like to do with your life? What are you going to do to make your wishes come true?

▲ **Would you like to be a musician?**

GOAL 4: Express Wishes and Plans

Reading

A  What would you like to do with your life? How are you going to do it? Discuss as a group.

I would like to _____ .

So I am going to _____

_____ .

B Derek Sivers has some surprising ideas about how we can achieve our goals. Read the article about his ideas. Then choose the correct answers below.

1. Derek Sivers suggests we NOT tell anyone about our _____ .
   a. goals
   b. thoughts
   c. opinions

2. People usually don't _____ their plans if they say them out loud.
   a. forget
   b. complete
   c. share

3. Being quiet about a life plan means the same as _____ it.
   a. explaining
   b. talking about
   c. not talking about

4. How does Derek Sivers say people feel when they share their life plans?
   a. frightened
   b. cheerful
   c. sad

5. If you say a plan out loud, sometimes your brain _____ .
   a. assumes it is true
   b. slows down
   c. thinks it is already done

WORD BANK

assume to think something is true
motivated have a reason to do something
psychologist a doctor who studies the mind
secret something hidden from others
trick to confuse or fool

TED Ideas worth spreading

Derek Sivers Entrepreneur

KEEP YOUR GOALS TO YOURSELF

The following article is about Derek Sivers. After Unit 12, you'll have the opportunity to watch some of Derek Sivers's TED Talk and learn more about his idea worth spreading.

Many people **assume** that the first and most important step in making any kind of life plan is to tell someone about it. This makes the plan seem real—like it's definitely going to happen. But entrepreneur Derek Sivers thinks it's probably better to keep it **secret**. He says that studies have shown that announcing a goal doesn't actually bring you any closer to seeing it come true. In fact, the opposite usually happens. People rarely finish what they *say* they plan to do.

Psychologists say that talking about our plans **tricks** the mind into thinking they are already done. People get happy, as if they have already achieved the goal. This makes us less **motivated** to accomplish what we would like to do. This is called a "social reality." The plan is definitely real, but it often doesn't develop into anything more than an idea.

So the next time someone asks you about your life plans, you might want to keep quiet. By being quiet, you may actually put yourself closer to your goal.

"Resist the temptation to announce your goal."
— Derek Sivers

143

If you want to achieve a goal, you should spend your time working toward it, not telling people about it.

Writing

A Help the people with their wishes. Complete the sentences with the correct plans.

save some money	invite her friends
have a family meal	find a good coach

1. Ben would like to take a long vacation. What is he going to to?
   He is going to _____ .

2. Helen would like to have a party. What is she going to do?
   She is going to _____ .

3. I would like to become a tennis player. What am I going to do?
   I am going to _____ .

4. It is our father's birthday next week. What are we going to do?
   We are going to_____ .

B What would you like to do with your life? How are you going to do it? Write a life plan.

Communication

I would like to be a teacher. I'm going to study every night.

A 🎧 Derek Sivers says you can still talk about a goal, but you should talk about it so it sounds hard to accomplish. Share your life plans with a partner. How are they the same or different? Discuss.

B 👥 **GOAL CHECK** ✔ **Express wishes and plans**
Share life plans. Is there anything in the life plans your classmates should NOT do? What should they do instead? Give your opinions and discuss as a group.

Before You Watch

A 🔁 Read the video summary. With a partner, try to guess the meanings of the words in **bold**.

While You Watch

A ▶️ Watch the video. Number the sentences in the order you see them.

____ Manat doesn't win.

____ Manat goes into the ring for a ceremony.

____ The fight begins.

____ Manat trains very hard.

____ Manat will become a champion.

B ▶️ Watch the video again. Complete the sentences with words from the box.

1. Manat comes from a _____ family.

2. Manat's coaches believe he will be a _____.

3. When Manat wins, he wants to send the money to his _____.

4. Manat doesn't _____.

After You Watch

A 🔁 Answer these questions with a partner.

1. Do you think Manat will get his wish to become a Thai boxing champion?

2. What do you think about the camp? Name positive and negative things.

Video Summary

Thai **boxing,** or Muay Thai, is a traditional **martial art** from Thailand. Thai boxers use their hands, elbows, knees, and legs. Manat is a 12-year-old boy from a poor family who is living at a Thai boxing **training camp.** He trains seven hours a day, seven days a week. He wishes to become a boxing champion. He works very hard.

family   champion   poor   win

On the Move

Elephants roam miles of grassy savanna
inside Queen Elizabeth Park, Uganda.

UNIT 12 GOALS

1. Use the simple past

2. Give biographical information

3. Describe a move

4. Discuss migrations

Vocabulary

▲ leave

▲ arrive in/at

▲ return to/from

▲ go to

▲ come from/to

▲ move from/to

▲ stay in/at

A Circle the correct verb in parentheses.

1. People (move | leave) their homes when they go to work.
2. They are going to (arrive | come) to our school tomorrow.
3. I am going to (come | stay) at Jim's house tonight.
4. At the moment, John is (staying | returning) to Toronto.
5. Children (go | stay) to school at eight o'clock.

Grammar: Simple past tense

Simple past tense		
Statement	**Negative**	***Wh-* questions**
He **moved** from New York to San Francisco.	I **didn't stay** in California.	When **did they leave** Germany? How long **did you stay** in France?
*We use the simple past tense to talk about completed actions.		

*Some verbs are regular in the simple past. They have an *-ed* ending. return—returned move—moved stay—stayed live—lived arrive—arrived	*Some verbs are irregular in the simple past. They have many different forms. go—went do—did come—came be—(I/he/she) was / (you/they) were leave—left

A Change the sentences to the simple past tense.

1. I live in Amsterdam. _____

2. They arrive today. _____

3. When does Jenny arrive? _____

4. Do you live with your parents? _____

5. I go to English class in the evening. _____

Word Focus

2012	↕	**for** 2 years
2013		
2014		
2015	←	**in** 2015

B Fill in the blanks using the correct form of the verb.

1. When did you leave Canada? I _____ in 2010.

2. How long _____ in Saudi Arabia? I stayed there for three years.

3. Did you live in Brazil for three months? No, we _____.
   We _____ there for three years.

4. When did you arrive in the United States? I _____ three years ago.

C Unscramble these questions and then ask them to your partner.

1. arrive at / When / did you / school? _____

2. to school / Did you / by bus? / come _____

3. homework? / your / do / Did you _____

4. home? / did you / When / leave _____

Conversation

A 🔊 26 Listen to the conversation. When did Abdul arrive in Canada?

Ed: <u>Abdul</u>, you're not <u>Canadian</u>, are you?

Abdul: No, I'm from <u>Syria</u>, but later my parents moved to <u>France</u>.

Ed: How long did you stay in <u>France</u>?

Abdul: Twelve years. But then I left <u>France</u> when I was 18 to study in the <u>United States</u>.

Ed: And when did you come to <u>Canada</u>?

Abdul: I came here five years ago.

B 🔄 Practice the conversation with a partner. Switch roles and practice it again.

C 🔄 Change the underlined words and make a new conversation.

D 🔄 **GOAL CHECK** ✓ **Use the simple past**

Have you or your parents ever moved? With a partner, take turns asking each other about the moves.

▲ Stanley Park in Vancouver, Canada

Listening

A 🔊 **27** Do you know these people? Write the names under the photos. Listen and check.

> Albert Einstein   Jerry Yang   Salma Hayek   Albert Pujols

Famous Immigrants to the United States

We say years like this:

1990 = nineteen ninety
2000 = two thousand
2014 = two thousand fourteen

We say *When **were you**/ **was she** born?* to find out someone's year of birth. The reply is ***I/she was** born in (1980)*.

1. _____

2. _____

3. _____

4. _____

B 🔊 **27** Listen carefully for the dates. Circle **T** for *true* and **F** for *false*.

1. Albert Einstein moved to the United States in 1933.   **T**   **F**
2. Salma Hayek was born in 1976.   **T**   **F**
3. Jerry Yang moved to San Jose in 1976.   **T**   **F**
4. Albert Pujols moved to the United States in 1990.   **T**   **F**

C 🔊 **27** Listen again and answer the questions.

1. Where did Albert Einstein go to school? _____
2. Who did Salma Hayek live with in the United States? _____
3. In what year did Jerry Yang start his company? _____
4. When did Albert Pujols become an American citizen? _____

Pronunciation: -ed endings

A 🔊 28 Listen and check (✓) the correct column.

B 🔄 Practice these sentences with a partner.

1. He moved to Peru in 1989.
2. They wanted to go to Egypt.
3. My mother cooked a delicious meal.
4. We walked to the beach.
5. I traveled from Buenos Aires by plane.
6. Kris wanted to buy a new coat.

	/d/ ending	/t/ ending	/ɪd/ ending
1. returned			
2. moved			
3. wanted			
4. traveled			
5. cooked			
6. stayed			
7. lived			
8. walked			

Communication

A 🔄 Read the itineraries. Take turns asking where and when Jane Goodall and Zahi Hawass traveled.

London, September 5th

Dar es Salaam, September 6th to 12th

Johannesburg, September 13th to 15th

Miami, September 16th to 25th

▲ This is Zahi Hawass, the famous Egyptologist.

Where did he go first?

When did Jane Goodall leave London?

Cairo, April 29th

Washington, D.C., April 29th to May 3rd

Paris, May 4th to 10th

Edinburgh, May 10th to 11th

▲ This is Jane Goodall, the famous chimpanzee expert.

B 🔄 **GOAL CHECK** ✔ **Give biographical information**

Think of a friend or family member who has moved a lot in the past. Tell a partner where and when he or she moved.

Language Expansion: Preparing to move

▲ close the bank account

▲ stop the mail

▲ have a going-away party

▲ get a passport

▲ pack

▲ sell the house

▲ buy the tickets

▲ sell the car

A Imagine that you and your family are moving to another country. Write sentences about what you did and didn't do from the checklist.

☑ sell the house   ☐ get a passport   ☐ have a going-away party

☑ buy the tickets   ☑ sell the car   ☑ stop the mail

☐ pack   ☐ close the bank account

1. _____
2. _____
3. _____
4. _____
5. _____
6. _____
7. _____
8. _____

Word Focus

Note the following irregular past tenses:

sell—sold   buy—bought
get—got   have—had

Some verbs have a spelling change in the past tense.
stop—stopped

Grammar: Simple past tense—*Yes/No* questions

Simple past tense	
Yes/No **questions**	**Short answers**
Did they **return** to New York?	Yes, they **did.** No, they **didn't.**

A Unscramble the words to write questions.

1. going-away party? have a Did they _____

2. you the sell house? Did _____

3. Did the tickets? Ian buy _____

4. close the Did we windows? _____

5. pack they their Did things? _____

B 🔄 Complete the sentences. Practice them with a partner.

1. A: _____ buy the tickets?   **B:** Yes, I _____ .

2. A: Did you _____ ?   **B:** No, I _____ .

3. A: Did they _____ the house?   **B:** No, _____ .

C 🔄 With a partner, take turns asking questions about the checklist on page 152.

> Did you sell your car?

Conversation

A 🔊 29 Where are David and Liana moving? Listen to the conversation.

David: Did you <u>get the tickets</u>?
Liana: Yes, I did. Here they are.
David: Great!
Liana: And did you <u>sell the car</u>?
David: Yes, I did. I got <u>$3,000</u> for it.
Liana: Wow! <u>Now I can buy some nice warm clothes</u> for <u>Canada</u>.

B 🔄 Practice the conversation with a partner. Switch roles and practice it again.

C 🔄 Change the underlined words and make a new conversation.

D 👥 **GOAL CHECK** ✔ **Describe a move**

Yesterday Jack got a great job in a new city, but now he has to move . . . this weekend! In a group, take turns asking questions like: What did he already do? What didn't he do yet? Use your imagination.

▲ It looks like he's already packed!

These people are from the Congo, in Africa. They left their homes during the war, but now they are returning.

D | GOAL 4: Discuss Migrations

Reading

A At some time in the past, your ancestors moved to your country. Maybe it was 100 years ago; maybe it was 100,000 years ago. Where did they come from?

B Read. Underline the regular verbs and circle the irregular verbs in the simple past tense.

C Answer the questions.

1. Where did humans first appear?

   _____

   _____

2. Where did they migrate to first?

   _____

   _____

3. How did Europeans move across the United States?

   _____

   _____

4. Give an example of economic migration.

   _____

   _____

5. Give an example of forced migration.

   _____

   _____

Word Focus

economic = about money

forced = when something is not your choice

migrate = to move from one place to another

war = a fight

HUMAN **MIGRATION**

We think that modern humans appeared in Africa about 200,000 years ago. But they didn't stay in Africa. They **migrated** out of Africa to the Middle East and then to the rest of the world. Throughout history, people have migrated from one place to another. People, it seems, like to move.

Since the 17th century, many European people moved from Europe to the Americas. They left Spain and Portugal and moved to South America.

Many Northern Europeans migrated to North America. In the United States, most people arrived in New York. Some stayed on the East Coast, but many people migrated to the West Coast using wagon trains.

So, why do people move? First, there is **economic** migration. People move to find work and a good life. Second, there is **forced** migration. People move because of **wars;** it is not safe to stay in their homes.

Of course, many people don't migrate. They stay in the same place all their lives. But people like to visit different countries on their vacations. People, it seems, just like to move.

Maya Bay, Thailand

▲ Rome, Italy

▲ Rio de Janeiro, Brazil

Did you choose Italy?

visited	went
stayed	left
arrived	

Communication

A 🔁 With a partner, read the travel options. Choose one together.

> **Option A   Three weeks in Thailand and Cambodia**
> Archaeology and relaxation! 21-day guided tour includes Ayutthaya,
> Angkor, and many beautiful beaches and islands.
>
> **Option B   Summer in Italy**
> Learn Italian! Live with an Italian family in Rome for ten weeks.
> Learn about Italy's history, food, and language.
>
> **Option C   A year in Brazil**
> Foreign workers welcome to work at the Olympics and World Cup!
> Possible opportunity to settle permanently if interested.

B 👥 In a group, talk about what you have to do to prepare for your trip.

Writing

A 👥 As a group, write an e-mail to a friend about your trip. Use the verbs
in the box.

B 👥 **GOAL CHECK** ✔ **Discuss migrations**

Animals also migrate. Which animals migrate? Where do they migrate
to and from? Why do they migrate?

Before You Watch

A Complete the sentences with words from the box. Use your dictionary.

> spectacle   forest
> fragile   environment
> disaster   logging
> destroy   preserve

1. Monarch butterflies are very _____. Cold temperatures can kill them.

2. The monarch migration is very beautiful. It is a _____.

3. Monarch butterflies migrate to a _____ in Mexico.

4. _____, or cutting down trees, is going to _____ the forest.

5. Governments and organizations want to _____ the forest.

6. Millions of monarchs will die without their natural _____.

   It will be a _____.

While You Watch

A ▶ Watch the video. Circle **T** for *true* and **F** for *false*.

1. Monarch butterflies migrate from Canada to Mexico every year.   **T   F**
2. The butterflies are very strong.   **T   F**
3. Trees do not protect the butterflies.   **T   F**
3. Loggers cut down the trees and destroy the forest.   **T   F**
4. The Mexican government is not helping to protect the butterflies.   **T   F**

After You Watch

A 🔁 With a partner, think of an animal or plant that has a similar problem in your country or region. Answer these questions:

1. What is the animal or plant?
2. What problem does it have?
3. How can this animal or plant be saved?

TED TALKS

Derek Sivers Entrepreneur
WEIRD, OR
JUST DIFFERENT?

Before You Watch

A 🔀 What do you think is happening in each picture? Discuss with a partner. Use *looks* to describe your ideas. Do you share the same ideas? Write down what you think in your notebook.

1.

2.

3.

4.

5.

B Look at the pictures from exercise **A** again. Check your ideas. Match the picture to the correct heading.

a. An infectious disease
b. A wedding
c. A singing lesson
d. Migrating to a new home
e. Lost in a strange city

> Derek Sivers's idea worth spreading is that you shouldn't trust what you think you know; the opposite may also be true. Watch Sivers' full TED Talk on TED.com.

C Derek Sivers is interested in the assumptions we make in our lives. Here are some words you'll hear in his TED Talk. Complete the sentences with the correct words.

WORD BANK
assumption something believed to be true
block an area between two streets
brilliant very intelligent or skillful
imagine think about and make a picture of
obvious easy to understand

1. Marissa is a _____ singer. She practices all the time.

2. Can you _____ how difficult it is to move to another country?

3. It's _____ that washing your hands helps prevent the spread of disease.

4. The wedding is not on this street, but one _____ from here at the Marina Hotel.

5. Your _____ is correct. Birds migrate to find food and stay warm.

D 🔀 You are going to watch a TED Talk about making assumptions. Think about an assumption you've made. Was it true? Discuss with a partner.

While You Watch

A Watch the video. Put the quotes in order. Write the number in the boxes provided.

> "Sometimes we need to go to the opposite side of the world to realize assumptions we didn't even know we had, and realize that the opposite of them may also be true."
>
> – Derek Sivers

☐ "There's a saying that whatever true thing you can say about India, the opposite is also true."

☐ "There are doctors in China who believe that it's their job to keep you healthy. So, any month you are healthy, you pay them."

☐ "Excuse me, what is the name of this block?"

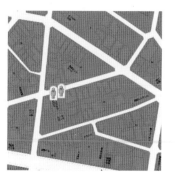

☐ "All of these blocks have names, and the streets are just the unnamed spaces in between the blocks."

Challenge! Can you think of an assumption that someone might have about your country that isn't true?

After You Watch

A Read the statements. Circle **T** for *true* and **F** for *false*.

1. In Japan, only the streets have names and numbers.   T   F

2. In the United States, the blocks have names and numbers.   T   F

3. In Japan, the houses are numbered by how old they are.   T   F

4. In China, doctors make money when people are healthy.   T   F

5. If you believe something, the opposite can also be true.   T   F

B Complete the sentences with the simple past tense form of the verb in parentheses.

1. The Japanese man _____ (ask), "What is the name of this block?"

2. We _____ (imagine) standing on a street corner in America.

3. They _____ (pay) the doctors so they could stay healthy.

4. It was obvious that he _____ (is) confused about the address.

5. I _____ (notice) that the house numbers don't go in order.

C Read the assumptions. Do you agree or disagree?

1. If a street doesn't have a name, it's impossible to find the address.   **Agree**   **Disagree**

2. You should only see a doctor when you feel sick.   **Agree**   **Disagree**

3. There is only one correct way to show the size and location of a country on a map.   **Agree**   **Disagree**

4. You only cough when you have a cold.   **Agree**   **Disagree**

5. People only move to find a new job.   **Agree**   **Disagree**

D Talk about the assumptions with a partner. Discuss whether you agree or disagree with each other.

You might assume that a hotel can't be made of ice. You would be wrong!

E1 Look at the topics in the chart. What do you think about each one? Make a list of your assumptions. With a group, discuss your assumptions. Do the other people in your group share your ideas?

Medicine	A headache:
	A stomachache:
Jobs	A dentist:
	A lawyer:
Celebrations	A New Year's party:
	A Thanksgiving Day meal:
Migrations	Moving to a new apartment:
	Moving to a new country:

E2 Research one of your assumptions. Is it correct? Share what you find with the class.

Challenge! From watching the TED Talk, what would you assume about Derek Sivers? Read about Derek Sivers at TED.com. Were your assumptions correct? Discuss with a partner.

GLOSSARY

UNIT 1

black: the darkest color; the color at night if there is no light

blond: having light, yellowish hair

brother: a son with the same parents as another daughter or son

brown: the color of earth or wood

children: people who are not yet adults

curly: hair that forms into curves or spirals

daughter: a female child

family: people who are related to each other

father: a male parent

friends: a person who someone knows and likes

grandfather: the father of one's father or mother

grandmother: the mother of one's father or mother

gray: a color like black mixed with white

greeting: something friendly you say or do when you meet someone

hair: a thin fine growth on the skin and head of a person

handsome: good-looking or attractive

husband: a man who is married

introduce: tell someone your name so you can get to know them

married: having a husband or wife

mother: a female parent

old: having lived for many years

parent: a mother or father

pretty: lovely or attractive individual

red: the color of blood or fire

short: referring to below average height

single: one who is unmarried

sister: a daughter with the same parents as another daughter or son

son: a male child

straight: in the form of a line without bending

tall: referring to above average height

wavy: slightly curly, rippled or undulated

young: not old, of few years

UNIT 2

architect: a trained professional who designs buildings and is often in charge of their construction

artist: a person who creates art, such as a painter or musician

banker: an officer or manager of a bank

big: large

chef: the head cook in a restaurant

city: an area with many thousands of people living and working close together

cold (adj): having a low temperature

country: an area of land which is a nation

doctor: a physician or medical practitioner

dry: without water or moisture

engineer: a person highly trained in science and mathematics who plans the making of machines, roads, and bridges

hot: having a high degree of heat

maize: corn; a plant with long vegetables covered in yellow seeds

numbers 1-101: (see page 18)

small: not large

taxi driver: a person who is the driver of a car for hire

teacher: a person whose job is to instruct others

wet: to have a high degree of water

UNIT 3

apartment: set of rooms for living in within a building with other apartments

armchair: a chair with armrests

back yard: the land behind and belonging to a house

bathroom: room with a bath and toilet

bed: a piece of furniture for sleeping

bedroom: a room for sleeping

bookcase: a piece of furniture with shelves, sides, and usually a back

chair: a piece of furniture with a back, for a person to sit on

closet: a small room for storing clothes, towels, sheets, etc

coffee table: a long, low table often set in front of a sofa

dining room: a room for eating in, usually with chairs and a table

downstairs: in the direction of or located on floors below

front yard: an area in front of the house

garage: a building where a vehicle is kept

garden: an area of land used to grow flowers and vegetables

house: building in which people live

kitchen: a room where meals are prepared, usually having a stove, sink, and refrigerator

lamp: any variety of lighting devices using electricity, oil, or gas

living room: a room in a house where people sit, talk, read, or entertain

microwave: a small oven which uses short frequency electromagnetic waves

refrigerator: a storage box with cooling and usually freezing sections for keeping food fresh

sofa: a long, soft seat with a back, arms, and room for two or more people

stairs: a set of steps going up or down

stove: a piece of kitchen equipment with burners, usually containing an oven, used to cook food

swimming pool: an area that has been dug-out and filled with water for people to swim in

table: a piece of furniture with a flat top on legs

TV: a box-like device that receives and displays pictures and sound

upstairs: in the direction of the level or floor above

UNIT 4

backpack: a type of bag carried on the back with two shoulder straps

bag: a sack, a container made of paper, plastic, cloth, etc. used to carry things

book: pages of words kept together with a paper or hard cover

camcorder: a hand-held video camera and recorder

cell phone: a small telephone you can carry with you

dictionary: a book listing words and their meanings in alphabetical order

DVD player: a device that plays DVDs

earrings: pieces of jewelry that are attached to ears

glasses: two pieces of glass or plastic that one wears in front of the eyes to see better

gold: valuable yellow-colored metal

jewelry: ornaments that people wear

keys: pieces of metal used to lock or unlock a door, start or stop an engine, etc.

laptop: a small portable computer

MP3 player: portable device that plays music

necklace: chain or string of beads worn around the neck

notebook: a book with blank or lined pages to make notes in

pen: an instrument used to write or draw in ink

ring: a circular metal band worn on a finger

silver: a valuable pale gray metal

smart phone: an mobile phone that can access the Internet

speakers: piece of audio equipment that sound comes from

tablet: a small portable computer that is navigated through a touch screen

wallet: a small, folded case used to hold cash or credit cards

watch: a small clock worn on the wrist

UNIT 5

check e-mails: to look at one's electronic mail

days of the week: (see page 58)

finish work: to reach the end of a work-day at one's job

get up: to wake-up and rise from sleeping

go to bed: the act of lying down in one's bed

go to meetings: the act of going to a gathering with work colleagues

go to the bank: the act of going to the place where one's money is kept

have dinner: to have something to eat in the evening

have lunch: to have something to eat in the middle of the day

make photocopies: to make copies of a document using a machine

meet clients: to get together with customers to whom a service is provided

start work: begin a work-day at a job

take a nap: to have a short sleep during the daytime

take a photo: to record an image using a camera

take a shower: to wash in the shower

talk on the phone: to communicate through a telephone

time: what people measure in years, days, hours, and minutes (see page 56)

travel: to go, journey

write reports: to write a document for work or school

UNIT 6

across from: on the other side of the street

airport shuttle bus: a bus used to take people to and from, or within the airport

art gallery: a place to display works of art, such as paintings, sculptures, etc.

between: in the middle of two things

bus: a large vehicle used to carry people between places

bus station: a place or building where buses pick-up and drop-off passengers

car: an automobile

hotel: a building with bedrooms for rent

journey: act of traveling from one place to another

library: a building which holds books and other reference materials for borrowing

movie theater: a theater where movies are shown for entertainment

museum: a place that displays rare, valuable, and important art or historical objects

on the corner of: at the place where two streets meet

park: an area of land where people can exercise, play, or relax

post office: a building where mail is processed

restaurant: a business that serves food

subway: a public transportation system with trains that run underground

supermarket: a large store offering food and general household items

taxi: a car with a driver for hire

tourist office: a center that gives information to visitors or travelers

train: a line of vehicles, such as railroad cars pulled by a locomotive

train station: a place or building, where trains pick-up and drop-off their passengers

turn (left/right): change direction

UNIT 7

cooking: preparing and serving food

free time: time not spent working or in school

going for a walk: the act of taking a walk outdoors

going to the movies: the act of watching a film in a movie theater

ice skate: to move over ice with ice skates

listening to music: to use our sense of hearing in order to enjoy music

play football: play a sport played by two 11-person teams, using an oval ball. In order to win one must pass or run the ball over the opponent's line

play golf: play an outdoors game in which people hit a small hard ball with a stick into a hole

play soccer: play a sport of two teams of 11 players, who kick a round ball into goals

play tennis: play a game on a court with two or four players who use rackets to hit the ball over a net

playing the guitar: using an instrument with six strings to make music

reading: to see and understand words in a book or magazine

shopping: the act of buying items at stores or online

ski: the sport of sliding down or across snowy surfaces on skis

sports: games that require physical skill

swim: to move through water by moving parts of the body

play volleyball: playing a sport played with players on each side of a net who score points by hitting the ball to the ground on the opponents' side

watching TV: the act of viewing the television

UNIT 8

beige: a light-brown color

black: the darkest color; the color at night if there is no light

blouse: a woman's shirt

blue: the color of the sky and the sea

brown: the color of earth or wood

coat: warm clothing worn over other clothes

colors: (see pages 96 and 100)

dark: close to black

dress: a one-piece article of clothing worn by girls or women

gray: a color like black mixed with white

green: the color of grass or leaves

hat: a clothing item which covers the head

jacket: a short coat

jeans: informal pants made of denim

light: close to white

orange: a color between red and yellow

pants: a piece of clothing that covers the legs

pink: a color between red and white

purple: a color between red and blue

red: the color of blood or fire

scarf: a piece of cloth worn around the neck

shirt: a piece of clothing worn on the upper body

shoes: a covering for the foot

skirt: a piece of women's clothing that covers the waist, hips, and part of the legs

socks: a piece of cloth worn over the foot and under a shoe

sweater: a warm piece of clothing worn over the upper body

tie: a piece of cloth worn by men around the neck for formal occasions

t-shirt: a short-sleeved shirt worn over the upper body

white: the complete lack of color, or the lightest of all colors

yellow: the color of a lemon or the sun

UNIT 9

apple: a round fruit with red, green, or yellow skin and firm, juicy flesh

banana: a long curved fruit with yellow skin

bean: an edible seed of many plants

bread: a food made of baked flour, water or milk, and yeast

butter: a yellowish fat made from milk or cream

candy: sweet food made with sugar

carrots: long, thin, orange vegetables

cereal: food made from grain

cheese: a solid food made from milk

chicken: a farm bird raised for its eggs and meat

chocolate cake: a sweet baked food made from flour, eggs, milk, sugar, and chocolate

coffee: a hot, brown, energy-giving drink made by water and coffee beans

cookies: a small, sweet cake

eggs: round or oval-shaped shell made by a female bird

fish: an animal with tails and fins that lives in water

fruit juice: a liquid drink made from fruit

ice cream: a frozen mixture of cream, milk, flavors, and sweeteners

meal: food you eat

meat: the flesh of animals

milk: a white liquid produced by some female animals such as cows

orange: a round, juicy, orange-colored fruit with thick skin

pasta: food made of flour, eggs, and water, formed in many shapes and boiled

potato: round or oval root vegetables with white insides

rice: white or brown grains from a cereal plant

salad: a mixture of vegetables, fruit, or other foods, served with a dressing

steak: a large piece of meat or fish, usually about an inch thick

tea: flowers and leaves that are dried, shredded, and brewed into a drink

tomato: a soft, red fruit

yogurt: a thick, creamy food make made from milk

UNIT 10

arm: one of two parts of the upper human body that extends from the shoulder to the hand

back: the side of the human body opposite the stomach and chest

backache: a dull, lasting pain in the back

body: all of a person or animal's physical parts

chest: the front of the human body above the stomach

cold (noun): an illness, usually with a blocked runny nose, sore throat, and a lot of sneezing

cough: to push air out of the throat suddenly with a harsh noise

cough medicine: liquid medicine taken for a cough

ear: one of the two organs used for hearing, located on either side of the head

earache: pain in the inside of your ear

face: the part of the head that has the eyes, mouth and nose

fever: higher that normal body temperature

finger: long, thin movable parts of the hand

foot: the body part attached to the lower leg and used for walking

hand: part of the body at the end of the arm

head: part of the body that has the face, ears, hair, skull, and brain

headache: a dull, lasting pain in the head

health: condition of a body

knee: where a leg bends

leg: one of the lower limbs of humans and many animals, used for walking and running

lie down: rest or sleep

pain reliever: a type of medicine taken to lessen aches in the body

patient: a person receiving medical care

sore throat: a pain in a person's throat

stomach: the front of the body below the chest

stomachache: pain in the belly

toothache: a pain in a person's tooth

UNIT 11

acting: performing in plays or movies

actor: a person who acts in plays or movies

anniversary: a date that is celebrated because of a special event

birthday: date somebody was born on

education: teaching people, usually at a school

go out for dinner: eat the main meal of the day outside of home

go to a game: watch a sports event in person

go to the movies: see a movie at a theater

have a barbecue: to cook food on a grill outside

have a family meal: eating with your family

have a party: have a get together or celebration with family or friends

holiday: a special day where people do not work or go to school

information technology: using computers to store and analyze information

law: rules made by a government body that must be followed by the people in a nation

lawyer: a professional who practices law

medicine: the science of curing sick people and preventing disease

months: (see page 136)

music: the art of putting sounds in a rhythmic sequence

musician: a person who writes, sings, or plays music

nurse: a person trained to take care of sick or injured people

plan: decide what you are going to do

software engineer: a professional who designs computer programs

special: more important than usual

teacher: a person who teachers or educates

wish: when someone wants to do or have something

UNIT 12

arrive in/at: to reach a place or destination

bank account: money in a bank

buy: to pay money for something

close: to shut down or bring to an end

come to: to arrive at a location

come from: location someone was in before

going-away party: a party arranged for a person who is leaving

go to: move or travel to

immigrant: a person who moves to another country to live

leave: to go away from

mail: letters, postcards, packages

move from: leaving a home to a new house or location

move to: a change of home to a new house or location

pack: to place, wrap, or seal objects in a container for transport of storage

passport: a small book issued by a government to a citizen of a nation

return to/from: to come back

sell: put something up for sale

stay in/at: to remain somewhere

ticket: a printed piece of paper bought for travel

GRAMMAR

adjectives, 8
   + *be,* 8–9
   demonstrative, 45
   possessive, 5
   some and *any,* 109
adverbs of frequency, 60
how much and *how many,* 113
indefinite articles, 16
nouns
   countable and uncountable, 112
   plural endings, 28
   possessives, 46
prepositions of place, 32–33, 69
there is/there are, 28–29
verbs,
   be + adjective, 8
   be + adjective + noun, 20–21
   be + *not,* 16
   be going to, 137
   can for ability, 89
   can/could (polite requests), 97
   contractions with *be,* 5, 16, 19
   feel, look, 124
   have, 49
   have to, 73
   imperatives, 69
   likes and dislikes, 100–101
   present continuous tense, 84–85
   present tense *be,* 5
   questions with *be* and short answers, 9
   should for advice, 128
   simple past tense, 148–149, 152
   simple present tense–questions and answers, 60–61
   simple present tense–statements and negatives, 56–57
   simple present tense–*What time* questions, 57
   simple present tense–*yes/no* questions, 152
   would like to for wishes, 140

LISTENING

biographical information, 150
conversations, 5, 9, 17, 21, 29, 33, 44, 46, 49, 57, 61, 69, 73, 85, 86, 89, 97, 101, 109, 113, 125, 126, 127, 129, 137, 149, 153
descriptions, 6, 30–31, 89, 98, 126, 138
discussions, 138
interviews, 18, 58, 61
introductions, 5, 6
party planning, 110
telephone conversations, 86
walking tours, 70

PRONUNCIATION

and, 111
be going to (reduced form), 139
can and *can't,* 88
contractions with *be,* 19
could you, 99
-ed endings, 151
falling intonations on statements and information
   questions, 59
final-*s,* 31
numbers, 19
/iː/ and /ɪ/ sounds, 46–47
/r/ sound, 7
sentence stress, 127
/ʃ/ and /tʃ/ sounds, 87
yes/no questions and short answers, 71

READING SKILLS 10, 18, 22, 34, 50, 62, 68, 74, 90, 102, 114, 130, 142, 154

READINGS

Chameleon Clothes, 102–103
Different Farmers, 22–23
Families around the World, 10–11
Human Migration, 154–155
Jewelry, 50–51
Journey to Antarctica, 74–75
Preventing Disease, 130–131
Soccer–The Beautiful Game, 90–91
TED Talks
   Brilliant Designs to Fit More People in Every City, 34–36
   A Guerilla Gardener in South Central L.A., 114–116
   Unseen Footage, Untamed Nature, 62–64
   Keep Your Goals to Yourself, 142–144

SPEAKING

asking for/giving directions, 71
asking/answering questions, 19, 21, 29, 45, 46, 47, 51, 58, 59, 61, 65, 69, 71, 73, 85, 104, 113, 115, 145, 151, 153, 157
comparing, 35
conversations, 5, 9, 17, 21, 29, 33, 45, 49, 57, 61, 69, 73, 85, 89, 97, 101, 109, 113, 125, 126, 127, 129, 131, 137, 141, 149, 151, 153
describing, 7, 11, 23, 25, 31, 99, 127
discussing, 23, 127, 139, 155
giving advice, 129, 131
greetings and introductions, 4
interviewing, 19, 61, 88, 113
making plans, 110, 111, 139, 141, 143
ordering food, 109
party planning, 110, 111

phone calls, 87
role playing, 127
telephone conversations, 85, 87

TED TALKS

Derek Sivers: Weird or Different?, 158–161
Karen Bass: Unseen Footage, Untamed Nature, 78–81
Kent Larson: Brilliant Designs to Fit More People in Every City, 38–41
Ron Finley: A Guerilla Gardener in South Central L.A., 118–121

TEST-TAKING SKILLS

checking off answers, 31, 47, 52, 65, 87, 99, 101, 111, 130, 142, 151
circling answers, 10, 105, 148
fill in the blanks, 7, 8, 17, 25, 28, 35, 48, 53, 68, 69, 145, 157
labeling answers, 12, 44, 48, 76, 80, 117
matching, 9, 30, 37, 45, 53, 61, 73, 90, 94, 97, 113, 117, 128, 149
multiple choice, 74, 105, 157
ranking answers, 145
sentence completion, 10, 13, 22, 25, 29, 33, 48, 49, 53, 56, 57, 61, 65, 68, 69, 73, 76, 85, 89, 96, 109, 113, 125, 131, 132, 136, 149, 153, 156
true or false, 6, 12, 17, 25, 31, 37, 46, 50, 62, 90, 93, 102, 130, 133, 150
underlining answers, 7, 9, 154
unscrambling sentences, 5, 21, 29, 57, 85, 109, 141, 153

TOPICS

Clothes, 94–105
Daily Activities, 54–65
Eat Well, 106–117
Free Time, 82–93
Friends and Family, 2–13
Getting There, 66–77
Health, 122–133
Houses and Apartments, 26–37
Jobs Around the World, 14–25
Making Plans, 136–143
Migrations, 146–157
Possessions, 42–53

VIDEO JOURNALS

Animal Families, 13
Danny's Challenge, 93
Farley, the Red Panda, 133
A Job for Children, 25
Making a Thai Boxing Champion, 143
Monarch Migration, 157

Slow Food, 117
Traditional Silk-Making, 105
Uncovering the Past, 53
A Very Special Village, 37
Volcano Trek, 77
Zoo Dentists, 65

VOCABULARY

body parts, 124
clothing, 96, 100
colors, 96, 100
countable/uncountable nouns, 112
countries and cities, 20
daily activities, 56
directions, 68
electronic products, 48
foods, 108, 112
furniture and household objects, 32
greetings and introductions, 4
ground transportation, 72
health and illness, 124, 128
jobs, 16
leisure activities, 84, 88, 136
moving, 148, 152
personal descriptions, 8
personal possessions, 44
places in town, 68
planning activities, 136
professions, 140
remedies, 128
rooms in a house, 28
sports, 88
time expressions, 56, 57, 60
weather, 20
work and school activities, 60

WRITING

activities, 92
commas, 48
descriptions, 12, 36, 52, 104, 109, 132
diaries, 80
e-mails, 156
interviews, 51
job descriptions, 64
make plans, 116
ordering events, 76
paragraphs, 24, 36
personal descriptions, 52, 92
self correcting, 115
sentences, 92
topic sentences, 36
wishes and plans, 144

PHOTO

Cover Photo: Martin Roemers/Panos Pictures

2: (c) Martin Schoeller/AUGUST Image, LLC; **3:** (tl) (bl) (rc) Martin Schoeller/AUGUST Image, LLC; **4:** (tl) Jupiterimages/Photos.com/Thinkstock, (tr) Ron Chapple Stock/Alamy, (bl) © Stuart Jenner/Shutterstock.com, (br) Bananastock/360/Getty Images; **6:** (bl) © iStockphoto.com/Aldo Murillo, (bc) Hill Street Studios/blend Images/Getty Images, (br) © iStockphoto.com/j-ezlo; **7:** (rc) jf/Cultura/Getty Images; **8:** (tl) © iStockphoto.com/Gisele, (tlc) © iStockphoto.com/Vetta Collection/naphtalina, (trc) Henglein and Steets/Cultura/Age Fotostock, (tr) Tim Robbins/Mint Images Limited/Alamy; **9:** (br) Radius Images/Corbis; **10–11:** (c) David Alan Harvey/National Geographic Creative; **10:** (inset) Peter Menzel Photography; **12:** (tl) (tc) (c) (tr) Martin Schoeller/AUGUST Image, LLC; **13:** (tc) Jed Weingarten/National Geographic Creative, (tr) Michael Nichols/National Geographic Creative, (rc) © iStockphoto.com/EcoPic, (brc) © iStockphoto.com/skynesher, (br) © iStockphoto.com/Nealitpmcclimon; **14–15:** (c) China Daily Information Corp/Reuters; **16:** (tr) © iStockphoto.com/selimaksan, (trc) Craig Ferguson/Lonely Planet Images/Getty Images, (tlc) © Peter Close/Shutterstock.com, (tr) © Kzenon/Shutterstock.com, (blc) © iStockphoto.com/Casarsa, (blc) © iStockphoto.com/Gelpi, (brc) © iStockphoto.com/Pinopic, (br) Nicholas Cope/Stone/Getty Images; **17:** (tr) picturegarden/Photolibrary/Getty Images; **18:** (tl) © iStockphoto.com/bonnie Jacobs, (lc) © mangostock/Shutterstock.com, (bl) steve cicero/Flame/Corbis; **19:** (tr) Emil Von Maltitz/Oxford Scientific/Getty Images; **20:** (lc) © iStockphoto.com/c-foto, (c) © iStockphoto.com/gioadventures, (bl) © iStockphoto.com/michellegibson, (bc) © iStockphoto.com/traveler1116; **21:** (tc) Audun Bakke Andersen/Flickr/Getty Images; **22–23:** (c) James P. blair/National Geographic Creative; **23:** (tr) David Alan Harvey/National Geographic Creative; **24:** (tc) Mauricio Handler/National Geographic Creative, (tl) Steve Winter/National Geographic Creative, (lc) Joel Sartore/National Geographic Creative; **25:** (tc) Darlyne A. Murawski/National Geographic Creative; **26–27:** (c) Courtesy Alexander Heilner; **29:** (tr) Urbanmyth/Alamy; **30:** (tl) Jaak Nilson/Spaces Images/Corbis, (tr) Simon Battensby/Image Source/Getty Images, (lc) © Rcpphoto/Shutterstock.ocm, (rc) © PeterG/Shutterstock.com; **31:** (bl) © Thierry Maffeis/Shutterstock.com, (br) Image Source/Getty Images; **32:** (tr) © iStockphoto.com/simonkr, (trc) © James Marvin Phelps/Shutterstock.com, (tc) © iStockphoto.com/c-foto, (trc) © iStockphoto.com/adventtr, (tr) ©

iStockphoto.com/s-cphoto, (lc) © iStockphoto.com/tatniz, (lc) © iStockphoto.com/blackwaterimages, (c) © iStockphoto.com/Auris, (rc) © iStockphoto.com/claylib, (bl) © iStockphoto.com/deliormanli, (bc) © iStockphoto.com/eyecrave, (br) © iStockphoto.com/tiler84; **33:** (tl) © iStockphoto.com/CostinT, (tlc) © Juriah Mosin/Shutterstock.com, (tc) Stockbyte/Thinkstock, (trc) © iStockphoto.com/Chuck Schmidt, (tr) © iStockphoto.com/Stacey Newman, (lc) © iStockphoto.com/Chuck Schmidt, (rc) © Rodenberg Photography/Shutterstock.com; **35:** (C) Sheryl Lanzel/TED, (tr) Reed Kaestner/Corbis; **36:** (t) Xu Xiaolin/Corbis; **37:** (tc) Claudio Camanini/Flickr Select/Getty Images, (br) ©Dan Clausen/Shutterstock.com; **38:** (tl) © jason cox/Shutterstock.com, (tr) © Sean Nel/Shutterstock.com, (cl) ©Photographee.eu/Shutterstock.com, (cr) © blinka/Shutterstock.com, (b) © Elena Talberg/Shutterstock.com; **39:** (t) Sheryl Lanzel/TED, (bl) WALTER ZERLA/Corbis, (bc) Sheryl Lanzel/TED, (br) TED; **40:** (t) © IR Stone/Shutterstock.com; **42–43:** (c) Reed Young/Reedyoung.com; **44:** (tl) © iStockphoto.com/klikk, (tlc) © iStockphoto.com/JLGutierrez, (trc) AbleStock.com/Thinkstock, (tr) © iStockphoto.com/WendellandCarolyn, (lc) © iStockphoto.com/Floortje, (c) © Ian 2010/Shutterstock.com, (c) © iStockphoto.com/DarrenMower, (rc) © patpitchaya/Shutterstock.com, (bl) © iStockphoto.com/polusvet, (blc) © Nastya22/Shutterstock.com, (brc) © jocic/Shutterstock.com, (br) © iStockphoto.com/Artzone; **45:** (tr) Jupiterimages/Pixland/Thinkstock, (tr) © iStockphoto.com/borisyankov, (rc) © iStockphoto.com/cotesebastien, (br) © iStockphoto.com/cynoclub, (br) © iStockphoto.com/Anna bryukhanova; **46:** (tl) Danita Delimont/Gallo Images/Getty Images; **47:** (tc) Ira block/National Geographic Creative, (rc) © iStockphoto.com/Jamesbowyer; **48:** (1) vetkit/iStock/360/Getty Images, (2) © iStockphoto.com/Rouzes, (3) © iStockphoto.com/Nicolae Socaciu/marlanu, (4) © iStockphoto.com/4X-image, (5) Oleksiy Mark/iStock/360/Getty Images, (6) ekipaj/iStock/360/Getty Images, (7) © iStockphoto.com/Infografick, (8) Lusoimages/iStock/360/Getty Images; **49:** (br) Raul Touzon/National Geographic Creative; **50–51:** (rc) Sylvain Savolainen / Cosmos/Redux; **50 or 51:** Krista Rossow/National Geographic Creative; **52:** (tc) Pete Ryan/National Geographic Creative, (lc) Lisa B./Flame/Corbis; **53:** (tc) © iStockphoto.com/Nomadsoul1, (tr) O. Louis Mazzatenta/National Geographic Creative, (trc) B Christopher/Alamy, (rc) Buddy Mays/Encyclopedia/Corbis, (brc) © Koroleva Katerina/Shutterstock.com, (br) © iStockphoto.com/samgrandy, (bl) © iStockphoto.com/wwing, (blc) © iStockphoto.com/DNY59, (bc) Jakub

Vacek/Dreamstime.com, (brc) © iStockphoto.com/pjohnson1; **54–55:** (c) RANDY OLSON/National Geographic Creative; **56:** (tl) © iStockphoto.com/digitalskillet, (tlc) chris warren/CW Images/Alamy, (trc) © iStockphoto.com/RoyalFive, (tr) © iStockphoto.com/Mlenny, (bl) © iStockphoto.com/CharlesKnox, (blc) © iStockphoto.com/Diane Labombarbe, (brc) © iStockphoto.com/Leontura, (br) © iStockphoto.com/monkeybusinessimages; **58:** (tc) Joel Sartore/National Geographic Creative, (tlc) Joel Sartore/National Geographic Creative, (lc) Joel Sartore/National Geographic Creative; **59:** (tr) John W Banagan/Photographer's Choice/Getty Images; **60:** (tl) © iStockphoto.com/skynesher, (tlc) © Istockphoto/Michael DeLeon, (trc) © Andresr/Shutterstock.com, (tr) © Dallas Events Inc/Shutterstock.com, (bl) © Junial Enterprises/Shutterstock.com, (blc) © iStockphoto.com/Alina555, (brc) Fotosearch/Asiastock/Age Fotostock, (br) Jamie Grill/blend Images - JGI/brand X Pictures/Getty Images; **61:** (tr) John W Banagan/Photographer's Choice/Getty Images; **63:** (C) James/Duncan/Davidson/TED, (tr) Mark Daffey/Lonely Planet Images/Getty Images; **64:** (t) brian Skyum/Alamy, (c) C. Douglas Peebles/Douglas Peebles Photography/Alamy; **65:** (tc) Philip Pound/Alamy, (tr) © Johan Swanepoel/Shutterstock.com, (trc) © iStockphoto.com/GomezDavid, (rc) © iStockphoto.com/GlobalStock, (brc) © iStockphoto.com/Roberto A Sanchez, (br) © iStockphoto.com/Chagin; **66–67:** (c) Sungjin Kim/National Geographic Creative; **69:** (rc) Pawel Libera/Robert Harding World Imagery/Alamy; **70:** (tc) Oliver Lopez Asis/Moment/Getty Images; **71:** (rc) Images&Stories/Alamy; **72:** (tl) © Tupungato/Shutterstock.com, (lc) Jupiterimages/liquidlibrary/Thinkstock, (bl) © iStockphoto.com/amriphoto, (c) Frank Short/E+/Getty Images, (tr) Fuse/Getty Images, (rc) © Robert Pernell/Shutterstock.com; **73:** (tr) Gavin Hellier/Alamy; **74:** (b) Frank Hurley/Royal Geographic Society; **74–75:** (rc) Frans Lanting Studio/Alamy; **76:** (tc) Chris Hepburn/Digital Vision/Getty Images, (rc) Marina BW/Moment Open/Getty Images; **77:** (tc) Paul Souders/Digital Vision/Getty Images, (rc) © iStockphoto.com/barsik; **78:** (tl) © Andrey Zyk/Shutterstock.com, (cr) © sukiyaki/Shutterstock.com, (tr) © ILYA AKINSHIN/Shutterstock.com, (cr) © Lonely Walker/Shutterstock.com, (b) ©aragami12345s/Shutterstock.com; **79:** (t) (c) (tr) TED, (t) James Duncan Davidson/TED; **82-83:** (c) PAUL NICKLEN/National Geographic Creative; **84:** (tl) © iStockphoto.com/Lisa-blue, (tlc) © arek_malang/Shutterstock.com, (trc) © Toranico/Shutterstock.com, (tr) © iStockphoto.com/digitalskillet, (bl) © iStockphoto.com/TMSK, (blc) Xpacifica/National Geographic Creative, (brc) © iStockphoto.com/Deklofenak, (br)©

iStockphoto.com/IvonneW; **85:** (tc) RANDY OLSON National Geographic Creative; **86:** (tl) Kumar Sriskandan/Alamy, (tr) poba/Vetta/Getty Images, (lc) ©Peter Kim/Shutterstock.com, (rc) Cavan Images/Iconica/Getty Images; **87:** (br) Gunnar Berning/Bongarts/Getty Images; **88:** (tl) © Light Poet/Shutterstock.com, (tlc) © iStockphoto.com/isitsharp, (trc) © iStockphoto.com/lightpix, (tr) © Alan C. Heison/Shutterstock.com, (bl) © iStockphoto.com/Sportstock, (blc) © iStockphoto.com/pappamaart, (brc) © iStockphoto.com/Ina Peters, (br) ©Galina Barskaya/Shutterstock.com; **90–91:** (rc) Aung Pyae Soe; **92:** (tc) Christoph Jorda/LOOK Die Bildagentur der Fotografen GmbH/Alamy, **93:** (tc) Harry Borden/Contour by Getty Images/Getty Images; **94:** (c) J Carrier/Redux; **96:** (tl) ©Elnur/Shutterstock.com, (bl) ©Elnur/Shutterstock.com, (cl) ©iStockphoto.com/lepas, (br) ©Karkas/Shutterstock.com, (cr) ©iStockphoto.com/stocksnapper, (bcl) ©sagir/Shutterstock.com, (bc) ©terekhov igor/Shutterstock.com, (bcr) ©Ljupco Smokovski/Shutterstock.com, (cl) ©Roman Sigaev/Shutterstock.com, (cr) Roman Sigaev/Alamy, (tr) Tibor Bognar/Photononstop/Canopy/Corbis; **98:** (tl) Bill Lyons/Alamy, (tr) Jose Luis Pelaez Inc/blend Images/Alamy, (bl) Glow Image, (br) UpperCut Images/AGE Fotostock; **100:** (cr) Eye-Stock/Alamy, (2) ©iStockphoto.com/popovaphoto, (3), (4) ©Karkas/Shutterstock.com, (5) ©Karina Bakalyan/Shutterstock.com, (tr) Greg Dale/National Geographic;**101:** (cr) James And James/Stockbyte/Getty Images; **102:** (c) Chris Johns/National Geographic Creative; **103:** (tr) Harold Lee Miller/Crush/Corbis; **104:** (t) Asia Images/Getty Images, (b) Robb Kendricks/National Geographic Creative; **105:** (t) Peter Ryan/National Geographic Creative, (b) ©July Flower/Shutterstock.com; **106–107:** (c) Courtesy Peter Menzel; **108:** (tl) © iStockphoto.com/Minute, (tlc) © iStockphoto.com/Jan Gottwald, (trc) ©iStockphoto.com/joecicak, (tr) © iStockphoto.com/scorpion56, (l) ©Timmary/Shutterstock.com, (lc) © iStockphoto.com/kivoart, (rc) © iStockphoto.com/jabiru, (r) © iStockphoto.com/Magone, (bl) © iStockphoto.com/muratkoc, (blc) © iStockphoto.com/Kasiam, (brc) © iStockphoto.com/katra, (br) © Olga Lyubkina/Shutterstock.com; **109:** (tr) Jorge Fajl/National Geographic Creative; **110:** (tl) ©iStockphoto.com/Iurii, (tlc) © iStockphoto.com/karandaev, (lc) © iStockphoto.com/BackyardProduction, (blc) © iStockphoto.com/

Oktay Ortakcioglu, (bl) © iStockphoto.com/Roel Smart/smartstock; **111:** (bl) Mikael Dubois/Johnér Images/Alloy/Corbis; **113:** (rc) Dadan Ramdani/National Geographic Creative; **117:** (tc) Jupiterimages/Photolibrary/Getty Images, (tr) © iStockphoto.com/mrPliskin, (rc) ©iStockphoto.com/lissart, (brc) ©iStockphoto.com/wojciech_gajda, (br) ©iStockphoto.com/monkeybusinessimages; **114:** (t) Andrey Zyk/Shutterstock.com; **115:** (c) James Duncan Davidson/TED, (tr) 145/Eunice Harris/Ocean/Corbis; **116:** (t) © Alexander Raths/Shutterstock.com; **119:** (c) (bl) James Duncan Davidson/TED, (rc) (br) TED; **121:** (top) Ambient Images Inc./Alamy; **122–123:** (C) Xpacifica/National Geographic Creative; **124:** (tc) © iStockphoto.com/Fredgoldstein, (tr) © iStockphoto.com/Comptine, (bcl) © iStockphoto.com/DRB Images, (bc) Paul bradbury/OJO Images/Getty Images, (bcr) © iStockphoto.com/Xalanx; **125:** (r) David White/alamy; **126:** (t) Alex treadway/National Geographic Creative; **127:** (t) Ton Keone/Corbis, (bl) Chris Collins/Corbis, (br) Baerbel Schmidt/Getty Images; **128:** (tl) ©iStockphoto.com/Digitalskillet, (tc) © iStockphoto.com/Svetikd, (tr) © iStockphoto.com/Qwasyx, (bl) Josep Lago/Getty Images, (bc) © iStockphoto.com/Lartist, (br) © iStockphoto.com/Podfoto ; **129:** (tl) Orenzo Menendez/National Geographic Creative; **130:** (b) Paula bronstein/Getty Images; **131:** (c) Karen Kasmauski/Alamy; **132:** (t) Cory Richards/National Geographic; **133:** (t) Gerry Ellis/Minden Pictures; **134:** (c) David Bowman/National Geographic Creative; **136:** (t) Collegiate Images/Getty Images, (1) LWA/Dann Tardif/blend Images/Alamy, (2) Robert Nicholas/OJO Images/Getty Images, (3) brand New Images/Getty Images, (4) ©Monkey Business Images/Shutterstock.com, (5) © Lucky Business/Shutterstock.com; **137:** (r) ©Fototehnik/Shutterstock.com; **138:** (t) PETER FOLEY/epa/Corbis, (cl) © iStockphoto,com/DenGuy, (c) blend Images - Ariel Skelley/brand X Pictures/Getty Images; **139:** (b) Andre Vogelaere/Getty Images; **140:** (tl) © iStockphoto.com/Rich Legg, (tc) Baran azdemir/Getty Images, (tr) © Bikeriderlondon/Shutterstock.com, (bl) © iStockphoto.com/Keithpix, (bc) © Maureen plainfield/Shutterstock.com, (br) AFP/Getty Images; **141:** (tr) AUL TOUZON/National Geographic Creative; **143:** (t) Steve Silver/AGE Fotostock, (c) James Duncan Davidson/TED, (tr) ICH REID/National Geographic Creative; **144:** (t) BILL HATCHER/National Geographic Creative;

146–147: (c) JOEL SARTORE/National Geographic Creative; **149:** (r) Pete Ryan/National Geographic Creative; **150:** (tl) Alfred Eisenstaedt/Time & Life Pictures/Getty Images, (tr) Michael tran/FilmMagic/Getty Images, (bl) Everett Kennedy brown/epa/Corbis, (br) Lisa blumenfeld/Getty Images; **151:** (tr) Patrick CHAPUIS/Gamma-Rapho/Getty Images, (br) JENS SCHLUETER/AFP/Getty Images; **152:** (tl) moodboard/brand X Pictures/Getty Images, (tcl) © iStockphoto.com/NoDerog, (tcr) Cavan Images/Iconica/Getty Images, (tr) niknikon/istock/360/Getty Images, (bl) Jupiterimages/Photos.com / 360/Getty Images, (bcl) ©iStockphoto.com/Livingpix, (bcr) ©Peter Baxter/Shutterstock.com, (br) Alan Powdrill/Getty Images; **153:** (b) Sasha Gulish/Comet/Corbis; **154:** (c) Nadeem Khawar/Getty Images, (t) KAREN KASMAUSKI/National Geographic Creative; **156:** (b) Michael Marquand/Lonely Planet Images/Getty Images, (c) MATT PROPERT/National Geographic Creative, (t) DESIGN PICS INC/National Geographic Creative; **157:** (t) © Melinda Fawver/Shutterstock.com; **158:** (1) Media for Medical/Universal Images Group/Getty Images, (2) JOHN EASTCOTT AND YVA MOMATIUK/National Geographic Creative, (3) Cultura Asia/Gary John Norman/Taxi Japan/Getty Images, (4) Chip Somodevilla/Getty Images, (5) WILLIAM ALBERT ALLARD/National Geographic Creative; **159:** (t) James Duncan Davidson/TED, (bl) (bcl) (bcr) (r) TED; **161:** (t) Jonathan Irish/National Geographic Society/Corbis.

ILLUSTRATION

6: Ted Hammond/Illustration Online; **8:** Kenneth Batelman; **20:** National Geographic Maps; **25:** Bob Kayganich/Illustration Online; **28:** (top) Kenneth Batelman, (bottom) Patrick Gnan/Illustration Online; **32:** Patrick Gnan/Illustration Online; **36:** Patrick Gnan/Illustration Online; **44:** Kenneth Batelman; **48:** Kenneth Batelman; **56:** Nesbitt Graphics, Inc.; **58:** Kenneth Batelman; **68:** Kenneth Batelman; **70:** National Geographic Maps; **77:** Bob Kayganich/Illustration Online; **81:** Kenneth Batelman; **97:** Keith Neely/Illustration Online; 110, **112:** Bob Kayganich/Illustration Online; **124:** Ralph Voltz/Illustration Online; **126:** Kenneth Batelman; **148:** Ted Hammond/Illustration Online; **156:** Kenneth Batelman.